"Kylie Cheung is an activist's dream. Not only is she committed to helping us all understand the damage abortion bans can do, she empowers readers with ways they can be part of the solution. Her book is a must-read for getting informed, staying sane and learning to fight back."

—Lizz Winstead, founder of Abortion Front
and co-creator of *The Daily Show*

"In this searingly personal, gripping account, Kylie Cheung explodes the conventional wisdom surrounding coercion and abortion. This book is an important new starting point for conversations about the real meaning of reproductive coercion."

—Mary Ruth Ziegler, author of
Roe: The History of a National Obsession

"Cheung's writing has clear eyes, sharp teeth, gorgeous rhythms, and immense power. This is an urgent, unforgettable book."

—Hannah Matthews, author of *You Or Someone You Love*

"Kylie Cheung skillfully shows us how the U.S. wields its foundational systemic oppressions against marginalized communities, especially women, gender expansive, and pregnant people in the post-Roe landscape. This book is required reading for everyone, and even if you think the issues covered don't affect you, Cheung's incisive analysis, journalistic skill, and compassionate approach quickly dispel that notion."

—Lara Witt, editor-in-chief of *Prism*

"A searing indictment of both conservative and liberal politicians' adherence to capitalism, white supremacy, war and policing, and how they have left justice for sexual violence survivors and abortion access in the lurch. A must-read for all who care about bodily autonomy."

—Renee Bracey Sherman, founder of We Testify
and co-author of *Liberating Abortion*

"In a moment when pro-choice politics feels stuck on defense, *Coercion* offers a necessary jolt of clarity and courage. Clear-eyed and meticulously-researched, Cheung's book exposes the violence of abortion bans—and demands that we think bigger."

—Jessica Valenti, author of *Abortion: Our Bodies, Their Lies,
and the Truths We Use to Win*

Outspoken by Pluto
Series Editor: Neda Tehrani
Consulting Series Editor: Lex McMenamin

Platforming underrepresented voices; intervening in important political issues; revealing powerful histories and giving voice to our experiences; Outspoken by Pluto is a book series unlike any other. Unravelling debates on feminism and class, work and borders, unions and climate justice, this series has the answers to the questions you're asking. These are books that dissent.

Also available:

Mask Off
Masculinity Redefined
JJ Bola

Border Nation
A Story of Migration
Leah Cowan

Behind Closed Doors
Sex Education Transformed
Natalie Fiennes

Mad World
The Politics of Mental Health
Micha Frazer-Carroll

Lost in Work
Escaping Capitalism
Amelia Horgan

Make Bosses Pay
Why We Need Unions
Eve Livingston

Tangled in Terror
Uprooting Islamophobia
Suhaiymah Manzoor-Khan

Feminism, Interrupted
Disrupting Power
Lola Olufemi

Burnt
Fighting for Climate Justice
Chris Saltmarsh

Race to the Bottom
Reclaiming Antiracism
Azfar Shafi and Ilyas Nagdee

Split
Class Divides Uncovered
Ben Tippet

Coercion

Surviving and Resisting Abortion Bans

Kylie Cheung

PLUTO PRESS

First published 2025 by Pluto Press
New Wing, Somerset House, Strand, London WC2R 1LA
and Pluto Press, Inc.
1930 Village Center Circle, 3-834, Las Vegas, NV 89134

www.plutobooks.com

British Library Cataloguing in Publication Data
A catalogue record for this book is available from the British Library

ISBN   978 0 7453 5061 5   Paperback
ISBN   978 0 7453 5063 9   PDF
ISBN   978 0 7453 5062 2   EPUB

This book is printed on paper suitable for recycling and made from fully
managed and sustained forest sources. Logging, pulping and manufactur-
ing processes are expected to conform to the environmental standards of
the country of origin.

Typeset by Stanford DTP Services, Northampton, England

Simultaneously printed in the United Kingdom and United States of
America

EU GPSR Authorised Representative
LOGOS EUROPE, 9 rue Nicolas Poussin, 17000, LA ROCHELLE, France
Email: Contact@logoseurope.eu

Contents

Acknowledgements

Thank you to Neda Tehrani, Lex McMenamin, and the entire team at Pluto Press for believing in this project and working with me. Thank you to all the abortion providers, abortion funds, fearless abortion storytellers, changemakers, and survivors who shared your stories and insights with me, making this book possible. I also want to express my gratitude to all the loved ones whose support buoyed me through the sometimes brutal, solitary process of writing a book.

When I was a teenager, an act of sexual violence changed my life. Afterward, so, too, did reading about feminism, writing about feminism, and organizing toward my vision for a feminist society. Today, through my work, I strive to challenge the ways that we conceptualize gender, power, and violence—in the U.S., in places where the U.S. is facilitating colonial violence, in a patriarchal world where gender-based violence happens not because it is aberrant but because it is the norm. But that norm is not an inevitability. This book is written for survivors. Everything I do, I hope, is an act toward building the world that I truly believe we deserve.

Thank you for reading this book. Please consider supporting the work of the advocacy organizations named in its pages.

Introduction

In 2022, the U.S. Supreme Court overturned *Roe v. Wade* with the *Dobbs v. Jackson Women's Health* ruling, eliminating the federal right to abortion. This altered if not altogether tore the fabric of society for women and pregnant-capable people— that is, anyone who can become pregnant, including queer and trans people as well as children. But around a decade before this event, in 2013, a New York court issued a foreboding ruling on a controversial custody case. That case, *McKenna v. Miller*, involved Olympic athlete Bode Miller, who sued his ex-partner, Sara McKenna, for custody after she moved from California to New York for school while pregnant with their fetus. The New York court initially determined that while McKenna, a veteran and firefighter, "did not 'abduct' the child, her appropriation of the child while in utero was irresponsible" and "reprehensible."[1] The court granted Miller custody, ostensibly as punishment for McKenna's interstate travel while pregnant.[2]

Despite weaponizing McKenna's pregnancy to sue and retaliate against her, Miller had previously sent McKenna this text when she first revealed her pregnancy to him and asked him to accompany her to an ultrasound appointment: "U made this choice against my wish." He ignored her text when she told him she was moving to New York. Like so many controlling or abusive men who wield custody battles to flex their power, Miller seemed less interested in parenting than in punishing his ex.

An appeals court ultimately reversed the state court's ruling before the end of the year. But nonetheless, *McKenna* presents

1

a chilling example of how the legal system can be, and so often is, used as a tool by pregnant people's partners to control them. At the time of the legal conflict between Miller and McKenna, legal experts expressed trepidation about the case's implications for pregnant people's rights. "Especially with current political pressures to recognize separate legal rights for fetuses, there will be increasing calls on the courts to fault a pregnant woman for moving, to restrain women from living their lives because they're pregnant," Sarah E. Burns, the head of the Reproductive Justice Clinic at the New York University law school, told the *New York Times* at the time.[3] This amounts to reproductive coercion, which occurs when someone tries to control their partner's reproductive decision-making or punish them for their decisions, often to entrap them in an abusive relationship and punish or exert power over them. Over one in three U.S. women have experienced sexual or domestic violence, which is endemic across the country.

Frighteningly, the *McKenna* case isn't an outlier: Across the U.S., an alarming number of states currently restrict or outright ban courts from finalizing a divorce during pregnancy—similarly wielding pregnancy to bind pregnant people to partners they're trying to leave, and affording men leverage to exert control over them. Texas, Florida, Mississippi, Arizona, Arkansas, and California all have such laws, according to tracking from the American Pregnancy Association from 2024.[4] Texas and California allow exceptions for domestic violence, but these exceptions aren't explicit in the other states. In Wyoming, Nebraska, South Dakota, Indiana, Mississippi, Alabama, Maine, Delaware, and Hawaii, there may not be an explicit ban on finalizing divorces during pregnancy, but "judges will likely make couples wait until the baby is born before allowing a divorce."

INTRODUCTION

In February 2024, one Missouri Democrat introduced a bill to allow people to finalize a divorce during a pregnancy; the lawmaker, state Rep Ashley Aune, said she filed the bill because she'd heard from a constituent who wasn't able to leave her abusive husband while she was pregnant:

> Not only was she being physically and emotionally abused, but there was reproduction coercion used. When she found out she was pregnant and asked a lawyer if she could get a divorce, she was essentially told no. It was so demoralizing for her to hear that. She felt she had no options.

In an extensive 2022 report from the organization Pregnancy Justice on fetal personhood—a rising legal movement that recognizes embryos as children with rights, and consequently subjects pregnant people to state policing to protect those rights—the organization warns that for years now, "divorce proceedings have been a site of great contestation" over embryos and pregnancy.[5] Pregnancy Justice offers legal advocacy to people who face criminal charges related to pregnancy, which is an increasingly common phenomenon.

All of this is further complicated in a country where, today, state laws may force someone to remain pregnant against their will, even when this is directly, frighteningly at odds with their safety. This is the same country where the leading cause of death for pregnant people is homicide, often perpetrated by an abusive partner.[6] Close to half of states have enacted total or near-total abortion bans since 2022—in each of those states, a pregnant person trying to escape a violent or otherwise abusive marriage may be trapped, all during a period of intense vulnerability, when intimate partner violence may begin for the first time or escalate to become deadly.

In 2024, Democrats, who had idly stalled on the issue of abortion for years, ran on a half-baked pledge to "restore *Roe*." But despite this lackluster attempt at winning votes, far-right Republican Donald Trump was elected president for a second time. His right-wing, anti-abortion Supreme Court appointments from his first term from 2017 to 2021 had empowered the court to kill *Roe*, and, even before the November 2024 election, his advisers at a far-right policy organization called the Heritage Foundation created an agenda called Project 2025, which detailed how a Republican presidential administration could effectively ban abortion without help from Congress. *Dobbs* is just the beginning. As I write this in 2024, it's possible a national ban or something like it has taken form, with a sufficiently right-wing judiciary to uphold these policies. In any case, whatever action President Trump does or doesn't take on abortion, the end of *Roe* has been a horrific outcome on its own.

New research from 2024 revealed a direct link between anti-abortion laws and a higher rate of domestic violence-related homicide in impacted communities.[7] Specifically, these laws—known as TRAP (Targeted Regulation of Abortion Providers) laws—weaponize burdensome, almost impossible requirements to purposefully shut down abortion clinics, ironically citing concerns for "women's safety." In reality, the study, which analyzed data collected between 2014 and 2020, found that enforcing just one TRAP law on one clinic led to a 3.4% increase in the rate of domestic violence homicides in that state. The authors of the study noted that in this six-year period, an estimated 24 women and girls between ages 10 and 44 were victims of an intimate partner violence-related homicide that was associated with TRAP laws. Under these circumstances, it's hardly surprising that a tenth of people who have abortions do so to exit abusive, dangerous relationships; a third have experienced sexual abuse in their lifetime.[8] Abortion bans exacerbate the risk of physical harm all around: At the end of 2022, University of Pennsylvania researchers published a study that showed pregnant-capable people of reproductive age are at greater risk of suicide in states that severely restrict abortion. The study drew on 40 years of data that preceded *Dobbs*.[9]

In the summer of 2023, the National Domestic Violence Hotline reported that calls involving acts of reproductive coercion had doubled since the *Dobbs* decision the previous year.[10] In at least one case that the Hotline shared with me for my reporting in Jezebel, one woman living in a state that had banned abortion said her partner stole her birth control pills and impregnated her against her will.[11] In a survey published in 2024, the Hotline found that out of 3,400 respondents, 5% (about 200) of domestic violence victims said their partners threatened to report them to law enforcement if they had abortions, while 5% said their partners threatened to sue them if they chose this course.[12] Access to abortion has always been a pivotal step in safely exiting an abusive relationship—but in a post-*Dobbs* legal landscape that casts inescapable criminal suspicion on pregnant people's wide-ranging reproductive decisions, victims can be punished for the very act of trying to protect themselves. In July 2023, a Nebraska teenager was sentenced to 90 days in jail for self-inducing an abortion in 2022 before the *Dobbs* decision; the teen testified that she'd made this decision to leave an abusive relationship.

Pregnancy has increasingly become a weapon to be wielded against domestic violence victims—and those who help them. Even before *Dobbs*, Texas enacted a law known as S.B. 8 in the fall of 2021. The law allows Texans to sue anyone who helps someone access abortion care in the state for at least $10,000, opening the door for rapists and abusers to literally profit off their victims' pregnancies, and harass their victims' loved ones with costly lawsuits. Already, we've seen several cases of legal harassment from abusive partners aimed at women in Texas who allegedly sought and received abortion care. Shortly after the 2024 election, the most powerful anti-abortion organization in the state launched a recruitment campaign seeking men interested in suing their ex-partners for allegedly having abortions. Texas Attorney General Ken Paxton reportedly used such an operation to recruit an aggrieved male partner to divulge information about his partner's abortion to the state, launching a major lawsuit against a New York abortion provider in December 2024.[13] Around this same time, domestic violence shelters in the state reported sharp surges in pregnant abuse victims or victims with newborns seeking shelter.[14] Abortion bans present a crisis for victims of gender-based violence—particularly the most vulnerable victims: There have been several cases of underage rape victims denied abortions in their home states, forced to travel for care or, in the case of a twelve-year-old rape victim in Mississippi, forced to endure the brutality of state-mandated pregnancy and birth. In 2023, at least 105 minors had to leave Texas for abortion care, and at least six were children under 12-years-old, per the state's Health Department; child welfare experts said most of the minors were impregnated by rape.

This is just a snapshot of the everyday realities that *Dobbs* has imposed on pregnant people, children, and survivors in the U.S. In these first years after the ruling, the gruesome horrors inflicted by bans began immediately and haven't stopped: at least five confirmed abortion ban-inflicted deaths, per state maternal mortality committees and ProPublica reporting in the fall of 2024;[15] rising maternal mortality and case after case of brutal pregnancy morbidities from being denied abortions for medical emergencies; a ten-year-old rape victim forced to travel out of state for abortion, and the doctor who helped her harassed and penalized by the state; the twelve-year-old victim in Mississippi forced to give birth, her family unaware of the state's vague and inaccessible rape exception; children of "childbearing age" denied life-saving medications deemed "abortifacients" at local pharmacies; pregnant people jailed on suspicion of having abortions; surging rates of reproductive coercion perpetrated by domestic partners; an estimated tens of thousands of rape-induced pregnancies in states with abortion bans.[16] There's even a growing movement to wield anti-trafficking laws against those who travel out of state for abortion—for trafficking the embryo or fetus.[17]

This reality is entirely at odds with the very principle of reproductive justice, which demands that all of us have equitable access to the resources we need to parent or not parent in safe, healthy communities, with full agency over our bodies, health care decisions, and lives. Reproductive justice is an international framework adopted by Black feminists in the 1990s; just as it demands full, universal access to abortion in the U.S., the movement also demands, for example, Palestinian liberation, the ability to be pregnant, give birth, and parent safe from violent apartheid conditions and genocide funded and facilitated by the U.S. The precedent of *Roe* was never enough to ensure reproductive justice—that's because, as *Dobbs* has shown, a rights-based framework is tenuous, especially when decades of compromise and fecklessness from liberal politicians resulted in these rights being perennially stripped back for decades. Still, the dismantling of our reproductive rights has pulled us back even further to the unthinkable.

Abortion bans particularly target those with the least resources and agency under capitalism and white supremacy;

then, seeking and being denied abortion pushes individuals and their children even deeper into poverty.[18] This is their intended purpose: to police and control pregnant people and their reproduction, to feed cycles of interpersonal gender-based violence as a tool in the toolbox of abusers, to inflict economic subjugation and racial violence, to actively kill pregnant people—by denying or delaying their access to life-saving abortion care, or entrapping them with their abusers in a country where homicide is, again, a leading cause of death for pregnant people.

Still, amid all the horrific state violence imposed on women and pregnant people, we're told that protesting outside Supreme Court Justices' homes or confronting anti-abortion elected officials is the real violence, the real threat to safety. In the liberal political imagination, "abortion" remains a concept—not a material issue, not a health care service that can determine someone's entire future, even whether they live or die. The curtailing of abortion access functions in service of the economic interests of the capitalist class, as anti-abortion lawmakers have repeated time and again: forced pregnancy and birth contribute to an ever-existing, ever-growing, impoverished, and exploitable labor force. In a similar vein, economic marginalization is a central component of abuse.

After all, the medical bills associated with experiencing gender-based violence are alarming. A 2022 study analyzed national data from almost 36 million visits to the emergency room in 2019 and found costs for sexual assault-related visits averaged $3,551 for all victims, while pregnant victims faced an even higher average charge: $4,553.[19] The National Sexual Violence Resource Center estimates the lifetime economic cost of rape across all U.S. victims stands at nearly $3.1 trillion, including $1.2 trillion in medical costs and $234 billion in legal costs.

And for pregnant patients seeking the full range of reproductive health care for their safety, it doesn't help that abortion bans have upended the medical system. Several surveys since 2022 indicate that abortion bans have deterred medical students en masse from learning how to provide abortion or training to become OB-GYNs out of fear of criminalization. The threat of prison time for providing essential pregnancy-related services has shut down several hospitals' entire labor and delivery departments, some of which served isolated, rural communities.[20] Within two years of *Dobbs*, nearly a quarter of all OB-GYNs fled Idaho. Health care providers are being forced to leave their states altogether, consequently entrapping pregnant patients in life-threatening care deserts. The National Domestic Violence Hotline's research has shown access to an OB-GYN can be life-saving for domestic violence victims.

Victims who carry rape-induced pregnancies, and are either denied wanted abortion care or make the choice to have the child, can find themselves bound to their rapist for life. As I've previously reported for my 2023 book *Survivor Injustice: State-Sanctioned Abuse, Domestic Violence, and the Fight for Bodily Autonomy*, assailants can easily wield the legal system to lead years-long harassment campaigns, not just stalking and punishing their victims (and their victims' children), but forcibly remaining a constant in their lives. One woman I interviewed throughout 2022 and 2023 in *Survivor Injustice* recounted a decade-long, ongoing legal battle with the man who raped her by his own admission, and went on to abuse the child she conceived from his violence. According to one research letter, in 14 states that banned abortion between June 2022 and January 2024, an estimated 519,981 rapes "were associated with 64,565 pregnancies." Of these 64,565 rape-induced pregnancies, "an estimated 5,586 rape-related pregnancies (9%) occurred in states with rape exceptions," and "58,979 (91%) in states with no exception," with 26,313 (45%) in Texas.

Rape-induced pregnancies are common and despite the outsized amount of debate and political discourse about rape exceptions, victims' options under abortion bans are slim to nonexistent. In 2022, one Republican candidate for the North Carolina legislature proposed a "community-level review process" for victims seeking abortions in banned states.[21] Surely you can imagine how such a process would play out for victims in a society that's misogynistic enough to enact abortion bans in the first place.

The end of *Roe* in the United States has upended daily life for pregnant people and survivors, and created new avenues through which the state and abusive figures can collaboratively punish and control their victims. As we attempt to wrap our arms around post-*Roe* realities with the limited data available to us in these first years since the *Dobbs* ruling, it's important to recognize that none of this happened overnight.

Through almost a decade of writing and reporting on gender-based violence, reproductive rights and justice, and the legal and health care systems, and talking to vulnerable people caught in the crosshairs, *Coercion* is my best attempt to contextualize the deeper impacts of abortion laws, particularly on endemic gender-based violence in our society. In the first chapter, I detail some of the legal history that led to the *Dobbs* decision—namely, how state-level abortion laws eroded meaningful access to reproductive care and endangered pregnant people and survivors for years.

In the second chapter, I explore the life-or-death stakes of abortion laws, particularly for domestic violence victims. The third chapter lays out how abortion bans and the legal system have become a weapon in the hands of abusers, examining how all of this is possible through the legal system's ongoing hostility and violence toward victims and survivors. The fourth chapter focuses on interpersonal reproductive coercion perpetrated by abusive partners.

In the fifth chapter, I map how the criminal legal system is another avenue through which pregnant people and survivors are targeted and endangered, and detail a history of pregnant people punished by the state for losing their pregnancies. The sixth chapter builds on this context, detailing extensive violence and reproductive coercion in the prison system itself.

The seventh chapter examines how the U.S. health system empowers abusers and endangers victims and pregnant people. The eighth chapter zooms in on the most insidious facet of state abortion bans: so-called rape exceptions, and the mythology, respectability politics, and dangerous fallacies these exceptions rely on to make abortion bans acceptable in the cultural imagination.

I conclude by detailing the thorny histories that gave way to the current political landscape around our reproductive rights, and the pathways available to us to build toward a more just future. Our only viable path forward requires us to reject the watered-down demands and transactionality of neoliberal politicians' calls to merely "save *Roe*," and recognize the deep intersections of survivor and reproductive justice.

In the summer of 2023, *Time* reported on the story of a child in Mississippi who had been raped, impregnated, and forced to give birth at twelve years old. As a young Black girl, she was adultified by doctors who questioned how she'd become pregnant, and her case was neglected by the local police department. Her family was unaware the state's abortion ban offers a rape exception—though, without specifications as to how this exception could be accessed—and didn't have the resources to travel out of state. As a result, the girl—a child herself—carried the child to term, and began the seventh grade as the parent of a newborn.

The story of "Ashley" in Mississippi, the violence she endured first at the hands of her rapist, then at the hands of the state, and then, through the ongoing costs her family shouldered as a result of her rape, epitomize a reality that the American political ecosystem often distorts: Abortion and abortion legislation are a matter of life—agency over one's life, the ability to pursue a dignified, safe, and meaningful life—and death, with endless material consequences, particularly for pregnant people, for victims of both domestic and state violence, for those who are already most marginalized by white supremacy and capitalist oppression. Abortion bans aren't apolitical laws, philosophical policy debates—they're political violence.

In November 2024, the immediate aftermath of Trump's reelection gave way to a particularly vicious cycle of cyber-harassment perpetrated by male, pro-Trump trolls. They rallied around the slogan "your body, my choice," slinging it at mostly young women and feminists in comment sections, on social media, even in primary schools and in the streets. This tagline seemed to serve as smug, double entendre—inseparable from Trump's election, from his party's support for a national abortion ban, is his status as a legally recognized sexual abuser and serially accused assailant. "Your body, my choice" says the quiet part aloud: Abortion bans are rape; abortion bans are control; abortion bans are gender-based violence and subjugation. *Your body, my choice*. Abortion bans put abusive men in charge of their victims' bodies.

About two months before the election, I had an abortion. It was a blessedly simple process—or, at least much simpler than it could have been if I'd lived elsewhere—and I wanted to think about it as little as possible afterward. That became impossible with the outcome of the election. I say that not because electing a Democratic president would have solved the generational crisis unfolding before all of us, but because the psychic toll of being a survivor of sexual violence, of having had abortions, and staring down the reality of a violent man seizing full political control of my body is visceral and undeniable.

I've written and reported on reproductive rights and gender-based violence my entire adult life. What's happening now is unthinkable. In *Coercion*, I try to make sense of it.

Chapter 1

The New Post-*Dobbs* Order

On May 3, 2022, leaked documents revealed a Supreme Court decision that would upend, well, everything: *Dobbs v. Jackson Women's Health*. In favor of reversing *Roe v. Wade*, Justice Samuel Alito referenced a seventeenth century English jurist who condemned at least two women to be executed for "witchcraft," and advocated for marital rape as well as capital punishment for children. "Two treatises by Sir Matthew Hale," Alito wrote, "described abortion of a quick child who died in the womb as a 'great crime' and a 'great misprision.'" The reference was certainly . . . a choice—one that accentuated the archaic nature of a ruling that would effectively reduce pregnant-capable people to state-controlled incubators under the law. It also accentuated the deep-rooted state violence at the heart of *Dobbs*.

In the days and weeks after the decision leaked, my reporting for Jezebel led me to examine the work of prominent anti-sexual violence organizations across the U.S. I searched for any acknowledgement of the impending Supreme Court decision, such as strategies to address the inevitable impact that abortion bans would have on victims and survivors. I largely found gaping silence.

Rape survivors' bodies have always been reduced to ground zero in abortion policy discourse. One example: Survivors have become political props for useless debates about rape exceptions. Useless, because a majority of rapes aren't reported to police or authorities, as they must be to qualify for most state abortion bans' rape exceptions. Abortion bans are "an abuser's dream," anti-rape activist and educator Wagatwe Wanjuki told me at the time in 2022. "They provide another tool of control over another person, and create a culture that's distrustful of women, distrustful of victims."

That few national organizations offering resources and services to rape and abuse victims spoke out about the end of *Roe* stood out to me; it suggested separation between two issues that are inevitably intertwined. One of the few organizations that addressed the impending *Dobbs* ruling was the National Domestic Violence Hotline, formerly called the National Coalition Against Domestic Violence, which shared a blog post in May 2022 calling the impending Supreme Court decision "catastrophic" and warning that "abuse often escalates when a victim becomes pregnant."

Within a year of *Dobbs*, the first public case of someone sentenced to jail time for their abortion involved a teenager in Nebraska who testified that she took abortion pills in early 2022 to end her pregnancy and safely leave an abusive partner.[1] As I previously wrote, in the span of less than two years after *Dobbs*, researchers estimated that in just over a dozen states that banned abortion, about 65,000 rape-induced pregnancies occurred; potentially, tens of thousands of survivors found themselves in a predicament similar to the Nebraska teen's, vulnerable to be tied forever to their rapist, facing the implicit threat of intervention from the criminal legal system if they acted.

In the state of Oklahoma, which banned abortion after *Dobbs* and has the highest rate of domestic violence in the nation, advocates working in victim services quickly found that the state's abortion laws have put victims at greater risk. "We've had a few patients come in saying that [their abusers] just keep the patient pregnant so they can't leave," a forensic nurse administrator at the Tulsa Police Department told *Mother Jones* in March 2024.

Of course, even before *Dobbs*, the policy landscape surrounding reproductive health care in the U.S. had always inflicted terror and state violence on pregnant people and survivors. *Dobbs* arrived at the Supreme Court because of a lawsuit over an abortion law in Mississippi; the case concerned whether the state's 15-week abortion ban passed in March 2018 was constitutional. By the time the case made its way through the legal system and arrived at the Supreme Court, the court had been packed with far-right, anti-abortion justices by President Trump, who had said at one point on the 2016 campaign trail that there had to be "some form of punishment" for people who have abortions. Ultimately, instead of simply ruling that a 15-week abortion ban is constitutional—an outcome that also would have devastated access to care across the country—the Supreme Court determined that, as Alito put it, *Roe* "was egregiously wrong from the start."

Even with *Roe* in place, abortion access was tenuous. In *Planned Parenthood v. Casey*, a ruling from 1992, the Supreme Court upheld *Roe*—but affirmed that restrictions that didn't place an "undue burden" on abortion access could stand. Not only did *Casey* leave the door open for these restrictions, but over the next three decades, its vague language, paired with the shifting, increasingly conservative political landscape of the country, yielded a wave of anti-abortion laws and the rapid shuttering of abortion clinics.

The 2010s saw the acceleration of laws that banned abortion at certain points during pregnancy, or created medically unnecessary, politicized requirements and barriers meant to shut down abortion clinics and push care out-of-reach. For example, state laws could impose mandatory waiting periods before someone could have an abortion, or force abortion seekers to obtain costly ultrasounds, or require clinics to have contracts with nearby hospitals, which were sometimes Catholic or religious hospitals and would refuse to work with them. In 2016, the thinktank Guttmacher Institute reported that the last five years alone had accounted for over a quarter of all 1,074 state-level abortion restrictions enacted since *Roe* was decided in 1973.[2] At this point, already, an estimated 90% of U.S. counties lacked an abortion provider. In 2017, one study of the availability of reproductive health clinics and steadily worsening maternal mortality and morbidity rates showed that millennial women were worse off than their mothers.[3] (Per the study, the maternal mortality rate for young millennial women had more than doubled since the baby-boom generation, from 7.5 deaths per 100,000 live births to 19.2. That same year, a report put forth by the Center for Reproductive Rights showed states with more restrictions on abortion had higher maternal mortality rates.[4]) By October 2021, just months before *Dobbs*, Guttmacher reported that for the first time in history, states enacted over 100 (106) abortion restrictions that year alone.

All these barriers compounded with a range of oppressions for people of color, people experiencing poverty, people with disabilities, queer and trans people, victims of domestic and gender-based violence. Pregnancy will always be more dangerous for marginalized communities. Black pregnant people are three to four times more likely to die of pregnancy-related causes than white people, per the CDC. Communities of color are substantially more likely to be uninsured or struggling to make ends meet, which can make travel for abortion and bridging the significant logistical barriers to access abortion care—missed work, transportation, lodging, child care—impossible.

In September 2021, about a year before *Dobbs*, Texas became the first state to effectively ban abortion via S.B. 8. Citing medical misinformation,[5] the state claimed that an embryo's heartbeat could be detected at six weeks, banning abortion at this marker. This law is enforced not through criminal penalties, but civil penalties: Anyone who provides or helps someone have an abortion in the state can be sued for at least $10,000. The Supreme Court affirmed that, even with *Roe* in place, this law could stand. A wave of other states introduced identical bans in the early months of 2022. The right to abortion effectively died months before *Dobbs*. Nonetheless, the end of a federal right to abortion, federal recognition of some degree of pregnant people's agency as human beings, burst the door open for something pervasive and terrible: fetal personhood, the acceleration of the carceral system's war on pregnant people and collusion with the health system.

Criminal charges for pregnancy loss and self-managed abortion tripled between the periods of 1973 to 2005 and 2006 to 2020, from 413 to 1,331 cases, according to Pregnancy Justice. The reasons pregnant people have faced criminal charges over the years are varied and terrifying: surviving violence that resulted in pregnancy loss, experiencing stillbirth and "improperly" disposing of fetal remains (even as there are no universal guidelines for this), choosing to have a home birth and experiencing complications[6]—even just Googling medication abortion pills and later having a stillbirth.

About 40 states have fetal homicide laws that can be and have been misused by police to criminalize pregnant people for self-managed abortions or pregnancy loss in recent years. Ironically, these laws were originally introduced to protect pregnant people by discouraging high rates of homicide against them.

In the seventeenth century, judges in Salem, Massachusetts, also cited Hale's writing—to sentence 25 women to death for witchcraft. In the same text cited by Alito, Hale wrote in defense of marital rape, "For the husband cannot be guilty of a rape committed by himself upon his lawful wife for by their mutual matrimonial consent and contract the wife hath given up herself in this kind unto her husband which she cannot retract." It's fitting that his voice is baked into and inseparable from *Dobbs*, a ruling that compounded decades of state gender-based violence.

Post-*Dobbs* Horror Stories Abound

In the immediate years after *Dobbs*, the violence inflicted upon pregnant people has primarily been consumed and understood through spectacle. In July 2022, a ten-year-old rape victim from Ohio was denied abortion care for her rape-induced pregnancy because Ohio's abortion ban (which was active at the time)—like most post-*Dobbs* abortion bans—did not include a rape exception. The child had to travel to Indiana to receive care. Her doctor, Dr. Caitlin Bernard, spoke about the child's case without any identifying details to local media; she was immediately subjected to a political witch hunt by the state of Indiana as well as the state of Ohio, which accused her of not reporting the child's rape to the government, even though Bernard *had* reported it. Both respective state governments wielded the power of the law to surveil and harass Bernard for months. At the time, the ten-year-old child's story became a rallying cry among liberal, pro-abortion rights politicians, who inevitably found the child's innocence and pure, unfiltered victimhood to be a winning anecdote. Conversely, anti-abortion politicians questioned the veracity of the case altogether, by proxy, these lawmakers questioned the credibility and victimhood of a child rape victim. Even a *Washington Post* fact-checker initially wrote the ten-year-old's story off, too, citing lack of police confirmation and his claim that child rape victims who have abortions are "pretty rare."[7] Eventually, an arrest was made; still, the right continued to harass Bernard. Feminist author Jessica Valenti wrote in her 2024 book *Abortion*, "Why would a police officer's account, or state official's, be more reliable than the one from the doctor who was in the room? Are we really to believe that in a state where abortion is criminalized, government officials are objective?"

The Ohio case should have shown that no amount of horror, no perfect narrative of victimhood, would appeal to the moral integrity of anti-abortion leaders and lawmakers: They aren't moved by the suffering their laws inflict because, put simply, this is what they want. And, indeed, the suffering has been legion, in many cases, documented in excruciating detail.

In 2023, a group of almost two dozen Texas women filed the first lawsuit in the nation specifically on behalf of people who suffered from life-threatening pregnancy complications but were still denied abortions due to ambiguities in the Texas ban's stated exception for medical emergencies. The case, called *Zurawski v. Texas*, was named for lead plaintiff Amanda Zurawski. Their suit stressed that medical emergency exceptions are ineffective because doctors, faced with the threat of life in prison, don't know at what point they can intervene. This threat pressures doctors to take a more conservative approach—at the expense of the pregnant person's health and safety, as their condition can rapidly, fatally deteriorate without warning. Thanks to abortion bans, emergency abortion care is denied or delayed until patients are on the brink of death and sometimes forced to suffer long-term health ramifications as a result—if they survive. There's an argument to be made that hospitals, many of which have robust resources to fight back against costly lawsuits, have a moral obligation to provide abortions despite the legal risk; nonetheless, state laws shouldn't create that legal risk in the first place.

The Texas women included Samantha Casiano, who joined the lawsuit in May 2023. In March of that year, after being forced by Texas' abortion laws to carry to term a nonviable pregnancy that threatened her life, Casiano gave birth to a three-pound baby who died four hours after birth. Her doctors had told her that her fetus would be born without a skull and die inside or outside of her womb. Still, she couldn't get the procedure.

Casiano explained that she was unable to publicly share where exactly in Texas she lived due to safety concerns from an abusive relationship. Her identity as a survivor speaks to an important reality: Many people who seek or are denied abortions are survivors, and access to abortion is essential for survivors—sometimes to escape interpersonal violence, and always to escape the very state violence that is perpetrated by abortion bans.

At least one other plaintiff in the *Zurawski* case testified about surviving domestic violence: In May 2023, Kiersten Hogan joined the suit as well and spoke to reporters about her experience being unable to safely get an abortion for her nonviable, unsafe pregnancy in 2021. Hogan's story began in June that year when she was living in Oklahoma, entrapped in an abusive relationship, and found herself pregnant. "When I saw the positive result on the drugstore pregnancy test, I was certain that this would be my only chance to have a baby," Hogan said, recounting her history of miscarriages and a previous fetal diagnosis. But to move forward with her pregnancy, Hogan decided to flee her "toxic and abusive relationship," which she understood put her pregnancy at risk. "The second [the father] left [for a business trip], I packed all my belongings into a U-Haul and left. A friend of mine lived in Texas and was also pregnant and I thought I would be safe here. Things were looking up for me." But in September 2021, shortly after Texas enacted S.B. 8, Hogan's water broke at just 19 weeks. She was taken to the nearest hospital—a non-Catholic religious institution that not only denied her emergency abortion care, but monitored, surveilled, and didn't allow her to leave the premises. Hogan recounted being held for five days against her will by hospital staff so that she wouldn't leave to get the abortion she needed:[8]

All they could do was monitor my situation. They didn't tell me much about my son's chances of survival, but the one thing that did make clear, repeatedly, was that I should not leave. I was told that if I tried to discharge myself or seek care elsewhere, that I could be arrested for trying to kill my child. I wanted this baby, so of course I stayed. Every four hours, around the clock, they would bring in the Doppler monitor and check the baby's heart rate. If it was too low, they would make me get up and walk around. When I needed to use the bathroom, I was accompanied and watched and made sure that I didn't push. I was scared to even have a bowel movement because the amniotic sac was protruding. Even though I said I didn't want religious counseling, they sent a chancellor to guide me. They kept saying it would be good for me. The goal they told me was to get my son, who I named Amon Blake, to 22 weeks gestation, when he might be able to survive on his own.

It didn't seem possible for me. Four days there, no changes. Just the same routine. The same feelings of birth coming too early and everything somehow being my fault. We didn't make it two weeks. On the fifth day in the hospital, while using the bathroom, my son started to enter the birth canal and I was rushed to labor and delivery where I gave birth to him stillborn.

Hogan's detainment is part of an alarming phenomenon in this country: Hospitals, including non-religious hospitals, have a history of holding pregnant people experiencing complications against their will, performing unwanted procedures on them, and sometimes colluding with law enforcement to have them detained.[9]

Lead plaintiff Amanda Zurawski also testified before the Texas district court. After becoming pregnant in May 2022, the same period that the Supreme Court's impending decision to overturn *Roe* was leaked, Zurawski learned she was pregnant. But 18 weeks into the pregnancy, Zurawski experienced severe complications that led to a life-threatening sepsis infection, the permanent closure of her right fallopian tube, and the collapse of her uterus—an outcome that has since jeopardized her fertility, even as she still hopes to have kids. Zurawski is one of several plaintiffs who expressed concern about infertility as a consequence of being tortured by the state abortion ban. And in a cruel twist, the state of Texas used that issue against the plaintiffs as it tried (ultimately successfully in May 2024) to throw out the case: Attorneys for the state argued the women lacked standing to challenge the abortion laws because it's not certain they'll become pregnant and experience life-threatening pregnancy complications again. Their experiences with being denied care are "tragic, but in the past," an attorney for the state said.

Another plaintiff, Ashley Brandt, testified that she doesn't plan to get pregnant again after being denied abortion care while pregnant with a fetus with a terminal diagnosis, and forced to travel out of state for care: "I don't feel safe to have children in Texas anymore." The plaintiffs also spoke about how their harrowing, near-death experiences were rendered even more stressful by the threat of criminal charges and lawsuits. Zurawski told the *New York Times* in 2023 that even as she feared for her life, she "didn't even feel safe Googling options" as she lost her pregnancy;[10] another plaintiff, Lauren Miller, said at a press conference in 2023 that her doctors "were afraid they'd be arrested just for saying the word abortion out loud" and questioned, "Where else in medicine do we wait and see how sick a patient becomes before acting?" Miller's experience isn't an outlier: People in abortion-banned states have shared a range of similar stories of doctors handing them a post-it with an out-of-state abortion provider's phone number, or a paper listing out-of-state clinics, handed over face-down.

Through it all, the state of Texas maintained in court that the women's experiences reflected the failures of individual medical providers to adequately interpret the law, rather than a failure of the law itself. The state's written motion to dismiss the suit accused the women of trying to "conjure standing by imagining a future scenario wherein they might be harmed," erasing their experiences and reducing their gutting stories to hypotheticals. At one point, the state's motion to dismiss implies the women filed the lawsuit for monetary gain because one of them created a GoFundMe to cover the high costs of burying her fetus.

In May 2024, the Texas Supreme Court threw out their case altogether, overturning the decision of the district court judge who had originally sided with the women. The state Supreme Court ruling was unanimous. It could only be interpreted as Texas officials—yet again—dismissing pregnant people's lives, inevitably condemning many to state-sanctioned torture, infertility, and long-term health complications, even condemning some to death. By the end of 2024, ProPublica reported on three abortion ban-induced deaths in Texas, from 2021 and 2023. In a statement responding to the ruling, Casiano said, "I don't know how the court could hear what I went through and choose to do nothing. Texas lawmakers claim to care about protecting 'the unborn', but in reality they made my family suffer."

Zurawski is the first lawsuit of its nature, but in the months after it was filed by attorneys from the Center for Reproductive Rights in 2023, the Center has since represented groups of women in other states who say that abortion bans and the ambiguity of their medical exceptions endangered their lives. In September 2023, a group of Tennessee women filed a nearly identical suit; one plaintiff, Nicole Blackmon, said she suffered "physical and emotional torture" from being forced to carry a nonviable pregnancy for months after Tennesse's abortion ban took effect in July 2022. Blackmon was 15 weeks into her wanted pregnancy when she learned her fetus suffered from omphalocele, a condition that impedes the development of the fetus' abdominal wall and results in organs growing outside the body. She was unable to get an emergency abortion in Tennessee, continued her pregnancy even as it threatened her health, and ultimately had a stillbirth. She then had her tubes tied because of how traumatic her experience with pregnancy in Tennessee had been, and consequently, the state argued in November 2023 that Blackmon no longer had standing to sue—because she was unlikely to become pregnant again due to her tubal ligation, the ban no longer affected her, the state reasoned.

The Center filed similar lawsuits in Oklahoma and Idaho around the same time in the fall of 2023. In Idaho, lead plaintiff Jennifer Adkins learned in April 2023 that her fetus had Turner syndrome and other severe anomalies incompatible with life. She was still forced to travel to Oregon for emergency abortion care, and, fearing criminal penalties, her Idaho medical team declined to help refer her to a provider. Adkins accused Idaho's laws of "[putting] my life at risk and [compounding] my heartbreak," as she grieved giving up a wanted pregnancy. This particular lawsuit also argued Idaho's medical emergency exception should include risk of suicide. "Pregnancy can have significant impacts on mental health and trigger the onset of severe depression, psychotic episodes, severe anxiety," Nicolas Kabat, a staff attorney at the Center who was working on the case, told me when it went to trial in 2024. "For some women, there's no medication that's going to make that better, and they need to end their pregnancy to make sure they don't end their life or suffer other psychiatric symptoms."

In Oklahoma, the Center filed an administrative complaint with the U.S. Department of Health and Human Services in 2023 on behalf of a woman named Jaci Statton, who was told by a hospital to wait in the parking lot for her condition to worsen before they could offer her emergency abortion care for her molar pregnancy. Molar pregnancies occur when an embryo has too many chromosomes and can result in developing tissue becoming cancerous. Statton's emergency room doctor told her she was at risk of hemorrhage and even death, but that the hospital couldn't immediately provide treatment—because treatment for Statton's condition was an emergency abortion, and abortion is totally banned in Oklahoma.

During that week, Statton was transferred to three different hospitals. At the last hospital, OU Health University of Oklahoma Medical Center, she recounted being instructed to wait in the parking lot. Statton told NPR in April 2023,

> They said, "The best we can tell you to do is sit in the parking lot, and if anything else happens, we will be ready to help you. But we cannot touch you unless you are crashing in front of

us or your blood pressure goes so high that you are fixing to have a heart attack."

Statton and her husband ultimately drove to Kansas for the procedure. Within a month, she had to seek surgery to remove remaining cancerous tissue in her body.

As lawsuits like the Center's continue to work their way through the legal system, I'm left considering the words of Linda Goldstein, an attorney at the organization who pointed to a throughline in all its aforementioned cases:

> They show exceptions don't work—that's the bottomline. Even before *Roe* was overturned, these exceptions have always just been window dressing to make abortion bans look reasonable. The language is too vague and too difficult for doctors to be able to apply to save someone's life—and that's the entire point.

Abortion bans, abortion restrictions, any amount of state policing of pregnancy is state violence. The legal cases that make headlines, the medical emergencies, the stories of child rape victims, may be among the most overtly jarring, but they're the tip of the post-*Dobbs* iceberg. They're a preview of an increasingly pervasive everyday reality of pregnancy.

A New Era of State Violence

In addition to the most high-profile cases of pregnant people denied emergency abortions for potentially life-threatening complications, high-profile cases of other seemingly endless, brutal, and ostensibly unintended consequences of abortion bans have fueled the outrage cycle too. They are, similarly, an introductory glimpse of the full extent of violence that abortion bans and pregnancy policing are inflicting.

In the fall of 2023, a woman named Tara Rule filed a lawsuit against Albany Medical Health Partners, charging the largest hospital system in upstate New York with discrimination over the denial of her medication, stemming from an incident she spoke to me about the year before in September 2022.

In a series of gutting videos, Rule described being denied a highly effective medication to treat a debilitating condition called cluster headaches, because her neurologist told her she was of "childbearing age" and the medication could cause birth defects to a hypothetical fetus. Rule said she told her neurologist that she never planned to have kids and would have an abortion if she became pregnant. But recorded audio in her videos shows that her doctor, referencing *Dobbs*, told her getting the medication she sought is "trickier now with the way things are going." He said she should bring her partner "in on the conversation" on her medical care. Rule asked if the issue preventing her from accessing the medication was solely that she could become pregnant and, "If I was, like, through menopause, would [the medication] be very effective for cluster headaches?" The doctor said it would.

Rule's suit alleged that denying her medication because she's of "childbearing age" and prioritizing an imagined fetus over her health violates federal law—specifically, the Affordable Care Act's anti-discrimination provisions and the Age Discrimination Act. "Where are we drawing the line here?" she told me for my reporting in Jezebel. "Are hospitals going to require someone to share a pregnancy test, proof they're on birth control, get a hysterectomy, to get life-saving health care?"

Rule's experience isn't an isolated one: In a similar example of post-*Roe* concerns around the mere possibility of pregnancy impacting people's access to medication, several people who could become pregnant have reported being denied sometimes life-saving medications that are deemed "abortifacients" by doctors and pharmacists. Even before *Dobbs*, in 2021, a pregnant woman in Alabama was arrested and prosecuted for trying to pick up pain medication from her pharmacist to manage a chronic back condition, as police alleged she was endangering her pregnancy. Rule told me she's heard from dozens of "people who say they were denied everything from acne medication to chemotherapy for the same reasons."

Rule said she's long struggled to find helpful treatments, but the neurologist wouldn't even give her the name of the medication he referenced because "he was so determined to protect a hypothetical fetus." Her case shows how the mere notion of fetal personhood can be taken even further, Dana Sussman, a legal expert at Pregnancy Justice, explained to me in 2023. "What we're seeing is how this ideology can extend beyond pregnancy itself—the idea that if you can even become pregnant, then you can no longer make decisions about your own body or access medical care."

In the fall of 2022, a few months after the overturn of *Roe*, a 14-year-old girl in Arizona spoke to local media about being denied her medication, methotrexate, for her arthritis and osteoporosis, because methotrexate can possibly induce a miscarriage, and the girl, Emma Thompson, was of childbearing age. Thompson said the pharmacist who helped her at Walgreens "didn't look at my history" and "just denied my prescription because of my age." In light of Thompson's story, another Arizona woman shared a similar experience on social media: "Daughter on methotrexate till they decided not to fill her prescription yesterday. RA and Crohn's. She is in her 'childbearing' years," the woman wrote in a social media post from October 2022.

Methotrexate isn't the only medication whose availability has been impacted by abortion bans: In the days immediately after *Dobbs*, the Kansas City Health System paused its service providing free emergency contraception to rape victims, citing concerns about the legality of doing so under an abortion ban.[11] Months later, virulently anti-abortion Georgia Gov. Brian Kemp expressed openness to banning emergency contraception, calling it an "abortifacient"[12]—a sentiment shared by large swaths of U.S. Senate Republicans, who almost unanimously opposed the Right to Contraception Act in 2024.[13]

In the spring of 2023, Iowa Attorney General Brenna Bird paused the state sexual assault victim compensation fund's long-time practice of covering emergency contraception and abortions for rape victims. Bird, who ironically ran on a platform of "protecting victims,"[14] also successfully defended Iowa's six-week abortion ban over the course of a prolonged legal battle.

With the overturn of *Roe*, emergency contraception immediately fell under heightened scrutiny, as anti-abortion activists and politicians have either openly admitted they don't know the difference between emergency contraception (which prevents a pregnancy) and abortion (which ends a pregnancy underway), or outright conflated the two in an unsubtle move to eventually ban both.

To reject the Right to Contraception Act in 2024, Sen. Joni Ernst of Iowa baselessly claimed it would "mandate access to abortion drugs for women and girls of all ages," equating birth control and abortion at a time when states across the country have criminalized abortion. She introduced her own bill that would ostensibly protect a right to access birth control, but with a key distinction: "It does not include Plan B, which many folks on the right would consider abortive services . . . We want to prevent a pregnancy, not end a pregnancy." Months before

Senate Republicans blocked the Right to Contraception Act, Tennessee Republicans in the state legislature blocked a bill to codify protections for IVF and birth control from even coming out of a state House committee; tellingly, Republicans argued this bill would limit the totality of the state's abortion ban.[15] Top anti-abortion organizations that work closely with Republican lawmakers have been equating Plan B and abortion for years; they've often targeted college campus organizations that install Plan B vending machines, or backed insurance companies and employers that don't cover contraception for "conscience" reasons, because they conflate it with abortion. In the summer of 2024, the Republican nominee for U.S. Senate in Wisconsin conflated abortion pills and Plan B—and even compared both to failed efforts to regulate the "hard narcotics" trade.[16] In 2018, during nationally televised Senate confirmation hearings for Supreme Court Justice Brett Kavanaugh, Ted Cruz also suggested emergency contraception is an "abortifacient."

Emergency contraception and abortion, if the victim can't access Plan B in time, are essential health services after a sexual assault; survivors, including some who testified in 2023 before the Florida legislature against an abortion ban that lacked a rape exception, have likened forced pregnancy to a "second rape."[17] And on top of the trauma and physical brutality of state-mandated, rape-induced pregnancy, the material, economic impacts are staggering, too—after all, the financial ramifications that can follow sexual assault, with or without a rape-induced pregnancy, are extensive. Again, sexual assault survivors' emergency room visits cost an average of nearly $4,000, while pregnant victims face an even higher average charge.

These figures present an especially brutal reminder of the material costs and consequences of abortion bans. Inevitably, abortion bans have stopped people from accessing abortion care.

Still, abortions have continued, but often ensconced in massive, cruel, and fundamentally violent barriers to care—barriers that endanger abuse victims, that torture and imprison pregnant people within their own bodies.

In December 2023, Guttmacher Institute published a study showing that in the first half of 2023, one in five abortion patients traveled out of state for abortion care. In 2023, Illinois, California, and Florida (which would later impose a six-week abortion ban in May 2024, effectively ending abortion access across the entire South) saw the largest increases in out-of-state abortion patients. In June 2023 alone, Illinois—a beacon for abortion access in the Midwest—saw a 45.4% increase in the number of abortions provided in the state compared to April 2022. In June 2023 alone, Florida saw a 48.2% increase compared to April 2022. Over the course of 2023, almost 200,000 patients traveled out of state to receive clinical abortion care, Guttmacher reported. Out-of-state abortion accounted for over 15% of the one million in-clinic abortions that took place from January 2023 through March 2024—a figure that's more than doubled since 2020.

Abortion funds exist to help people afford abortion care and all associated costs, and they're spending substantially more money post-*Dobbs*. Italia Aranda, an organizer at Mariposa Fund, works closely with undocumented callers whose ability to travel for abortion is limited by immigration status. Because of immigration checkpoints scattered across Texas, attempting to travel great distances or out of state to get abortions can come at the risk of deportation or criminalization. Barriers to abortion aren't new for undocumented people, who are more likely to be uninsured or lack paid time off: "For patients who are undocumented, traveling in search of access to medical procedures has always involved risk of deportation for something as simple as a routine traffic stop," Aranda told me in 2022. But challenges and costs have exponentially grown due to abortion bans.

In 2023, Texas' Lilith Fund spent $1 million, the Baltimore Abortion Fund also spent $1 million, the Abortion Fund of Ohio spent about $1.5 million, New York Abortion Access Fund spent $1.7 million, and the DC Abortion Fund spent $2 million.[18] In 2024, Brigid Alliance—a group that helps provide comprehensive financial support for all travel and logistical costs for abortion, prioritizing those in need of later abortion care— shared staggering data revealing how much more demand has been placed on their work post-*Dobbs*. The organization told me that it went from supporting an average of 40 abortion-seeking clients per month in 2019 to serving 150 per month post-*Dobbs*. Costs to support their clients also spiked: From 2021 to 2023, travel-related costs increased 16% from $836 to $993 per client, and in that same period, average lodging costs increased 29% from $242 to $345. It hasn't helped that the average distance clients need to travel increased by 30% between 2022 and 2023, from 1,000 miles to 1,300. Brigid's director Serra Sippel told me in 2024 that the organization saw a "spike" in donations immediately after *Dobbs*. But many of those were one-time donations. "This is a long-term need. Spikes don't sustain our work for the long-term," she said. "Anger donations have diminished and decreased at a time when the demand for services has only increased, the cost of services have only increased."

One of Brigid's clients, Nancy Davis, learned in August 2022 that her fetus wasn't viable due to a rare congenital disorder known as acrania, in which part or all of the skull is missing. But, because Louisiana's criminal abortion ban threatens doctors with prison time, she couldn't find anyone in her state to provide an emergency abortion since the fetus still had a heartbeat. Davis, a mother of two young children, and her partner had to make travel arrangements to get later abortion care elsewhere. "When you're in a tragic situation like that, the last thing on your mind is booking tickets, research, finding a place to stay," Davis told me in 2024. Brigid arranged for Davis to travel to New York for her abortion in September 2022, and also set up child care, lodging, and a meal stipend for her.

A spokesperson for the Abortion Fund of Ohio also told me in 2024 that, in addition to funding shortages, their fund's work has been made more difficult and laborious because the landscape around abortion access is "so confusing and complicated, to experts and to everyday people both." Helping callers navigate this system can be exhausting, on top of the labor of balancing the fund's budget and trying to fund people's abortions. And, of course, sometimes abortion seekers aren't able to find them at all.

Compounding all of this, because of higher costs, longer travel time, confusion, and more barriers across the board, delayed abortion access leads to more later abortions—sometimes "five, six weeks later than someone wanted to have their abortion," Sippel said. Inevitably, the later an abortion, the "more complicated and more expensive."

At an anniversary event hosted by Brigid in 2024 in New York City, Jill Hartle, a South Carolina resident and former Ms. South Carolina, shared her experience turning to DuPont Clinic in Washington, D.C.—one of few clinics in the nation that offers later abortion care—for a procedure in 2022. She'd been turned away by doctors in her home state due to South Carolina's criminal abortion ban. Eighteen weeks into her pregnancy, Hartle learned her fetus was missing the entire left side of its heart. "Our medical teams were not even able to fully discuss options for care with us based on advice from their lawyers," Hartle recounted. She and her partner were left to rely on the expertise and financial support of Brigid's staff to travel to D.C. and receive the procedure at DuPont. "When people ask if what I went through was difficult, I tell them my trauma does not come from my abortion. My trauma comes from the 49 days I was forced to wait for it."

Matt Reeves, director of DuPont Clinic, stressed to me in 2024 that long before the *Dobbs* decision, "everything changed, really, with S.B. 8 in Texas." He explained, "We saw a surge in later abortions after S.B. 8, and then the combination of that with the aftermath of *Dobbs*," because abortion bans and "logistical nightmares" were "delaying when so many people who otherwise could have gotten care much earlier" were able to have abortions. When abortion occurs later, the costs of everything increase.

And then, there's everything after the procedure. "The problems, the complications, the costs [from abortion bans]—it's unending," Sippel said. She's heard of people who have lost their jobs from being forced to miss work to travel for abortions, from people who lost significant wages from missing work for abortion care, and consequently struggled to pay rent and cover other living costs. "It can set them back for a long time. The short-sightedness of imposing these bans, the impact it has on the economic infrastructure when so many people are going to lose wages, lose jobs, lose housing—the ripple effect is massive."

The ripple effect we're seeing now, of course, only scratches the surface. Extensive accounts of pregnant people subjected to near-death experiences and long-term health impairment; the denial of basic medications deemed abortifacients, even to children; attacks on contraception and sexual assault survivors' access to it; nearly insurmountable costs and barriers—this is only a brutal highlight reel of the most visible, horrific consequences of abortion laws, the most shattering material impacts on pregnant people and survivors' real lives under a new era of state violence. This is an introduction; this is a beginning. This is the setting, the backdrop and new political context in which everything else detailed in this book unfolds.

Chapter 2

Domestic Violence, Medical Violence, and Anti-Abortion Violence

In May 2023, a Texas man shot and killed his girlfriend after she returned from traveling to Colorado to get an abortion, because abortion is banned in Texas. Police reports showed that the man had strangled and assaulted her just days before killing her, and he acknowledged that he knew she was pregnant. He'd previously punched her in the face, giving her a black eye and bruises on her body.

According to Everytown for Gun Safety, 70 women every month are shot and killed by an intimate partner. It's not a coincidence that around the same time the Supreme Court decided *Dobbs*, the court also moved to lift restrictions on buying firearms, expanding access to guns for potential abusers. State violence compounds by design; abuse victims suffer the consequences.

The homicide in Texas in 2023 is one of too many such stories of pregnancy escalating domestic violence, ending in tragic fatality. In 2024, Molly Voyles, director of public policy at the Texas Council on Family Violence, told me the victim services organization's tracking showed 72 women were killed by their intimate partners when they were pregnant or within one year postpartum between 2017 and 2023. "Banning abortion care for survivors of intimate partner violence is anything but accommodating to survivor-centered services, threatening the safety of thousands of survivors as they try to restore safety, privacy and autonomy to their lives," Voyles said.

It's possible the young woman's partner would have killed her had abortion been legal in Texas, and she'd been able to obtain it in the state. It's also possible the added necessity of leaving the state for care made the abortion more difficult to conceal, worsening her vulnerability to violence, producing a deadly outcome. This is another material impact of abortion bans: extreme, unbearable physical violence; for some, particularly for domestic violence victims, the loss of life itself.

When the Texas man, Harold Thompson, killed his girlfriend Gabriela Gonzalez for traveling out of state to have an abortion in the spring of 2023, the horrific act of intimate partner violence came nearly one year after a similar development: In the summer of 2022, a Missouri man was sentenced to life in prison for murdering his wife a few years earlier. Just before she went missing, his wife had searched: "what to do if your husband is upset you are pregnant."[1]

Homicide, mostly by an intimate partner, is the leading cause of death for pregnant people in the U.S. Abusive situations are likely to escalate when someone becomes pregnant. Abortion bans force people in potentially unsafe situations to remain pregnant against their will, sometimes at serious risk to their lives—again, several states with abortion bans even prohibit divorce from being finalized while someone is pregnant.

In 2022, Rachael Lorenzo, director of the reproductive justice fund Indigenous Women Rising, recounted trying to support a Spanish-speaking caller who sought an abortion to flee a "violent situation," and had several young children. The woman asked only that IWR mail her an envelope of cash to help her travel to Michigan for the procedure, and not call her cell phone unless she first sent a text message. Lorenzo sent the envelope of cash, but within days, it was mailed back to IWR, and they never heard from the woman again. "It is such a sacred thing for someone to be so vulnerable with us, and to let us in on what's happening in their lives when they might be in danger," Lorenzo told me.

Emma, an organizer at the Roe Fund in Oklahoma, told me her callers are sometimes abuse victims completely under their abusers' control and surveillance. Her state has the highest domestic violence rate in the nation. "It makes it even harder, on top of the ban, when you don't have control over your money, or have a car, or have a schedule or location or your mail are being watched, cell phone is being watched—that makes it nearly impossible," Emma said. Domestic violence advocacy workers sometimes connect their clients to Roe Fund, but Emma says she worries that many victims who would otherwise seek abortion care may be too afraid of legal risk or being reported to ask their advocates for help, which means the victims who are referred to her are just a fraction of those who might need abortions. Many don't even know help is available to them at all.

Emma takes all privacy and security precautions possible when communicating with callers, but still constantly struggles with the fear that "I'm making a woman even more endangered—is this phone call or text to them going to create even more problems?" She continued, "I don't think people realize how precarious this all is. For some people, you're basically risking your life to try to make an appointment."

Recall that, about two years after *Dobbs*, a new study showed a direct link between anti-abortion TRAP laws and higher rates of intimate partner violence related homicide, even as anti-abortion lawmakers ironically justified TRAP laws as a necessity for "women's safety." Between 2014 and 2020, that study estimated 24 women and girls of reproductive age were victims of an intimate partner violence-related homicide associated with TRAP laws.

"Survivors are being trapped by these abortion laws," Marrium Durrani, vice president of policy at the National Domestic Violence Hotline, told me in 2024 when the study was published. "In this really terrible new landscape, it's only going to . . . cause more death, more violence targeting people who are in abusive relationships." She also raised previous research put forth in the landmark Turnaway Study, a groundbreaking, longitudinal research project by University of California, San Francisco researchers assessing the enduring impacts of being denied wanted abortion care. The study showed that people who are denied abortion are at a significantly greater risk of long-term domestic violence. "You might find people tied to their abusers for much longer if they have children with them, creating heightened, longer-term danger," Durrani said.

Rita Smith, vice president of external relations at the direct services organization Domestic Shelters, told me that it will take years to begin to comprehend the full extent of gendered violence and death inflicted by abortion bans since *Dobbs*: "Criminal justice data is often lagging, so we may not fully see the impact of these laws on domestic violence victims for years, but I would be surprised if we don't see an increase in the number of domestic violence homicides during this time, in abortion-restrictive states." Between confusion about when hospitals can act to save pregnant people's lives and, as the May 2024 study shows, greater exposure to intimate partner violence homicide in connection with abortion restrictions, Smith argued that we're in the middle of a reckoning: "We're seeing a cultural shift in what the value of women's lives is."

The Life-or-Death Stakes of Abortion Bans

When lawmakers ban the health service that's a lifeline for domestic violence victims, a lifeline for people experiencing severe pregnancy complications, a lifeline for people who don't consent to being pregnant, this has the same impact and toll as violent men and abusive partners physically attacking their pregnant victims. Abortion bans are gender-based violence. By the end of 2024, ProPublica reported the confirmed deaths of five women—three in Texas and two in Georgia—that resulted from their states' respective abortion bans. In Georgia, shortly after the state's ban took effect in 2022, Amber Nicole Thurman and Candi Miller, two Black mothers, died after experiencing complications with medication abortions and being unable to receive a simple emergency abortion procedure in a timely manner. One hospital waited 20 hours to give Thurman an emergency abortion, at which point, she'd contracted sepsis and died during the procedure. Miller, meanwhile, was too afraid to go to the hospital as she experienced complications from a medication abortion, because she feared she could go to prison under Georgia's abortion law, even though the law only explicitly criminalizes abortion providers. Miller, too, developed sepsis and died.

In Texas, Honduran immigrant Josseli Barnica died of sepsis because doctors waited 40 hours for her fetus' heartbeat to stop before providing an emergency abortion to safely complete her miscarriage. Her death came just days after S.B. 8, the state's "bounty hunter" abortion ban, took effect in 2021. Around the same time, three Texas hospitals turned away 18-year-old Nevaeh

Crain as she suffered from pregnancy complications; she died from sepsis within hours of arriving at the third hospital. And in 2023, Porsha Ngumezi, a mother of two young sons, also died when her condition rapidly deteriorated, and the hospital declined to perform an emergency abortion to stop her hemorrhaging as she miscarried. "We all know pregnancies can come out beautifully or horribly," Ngumezi's husband, Hope, told ProPublica. "Instead of putting laws in place to make pregnancies safer, we created laws that put them back in danger."

Each of these women's lives contained whole universes; they had futures, they had children or other loved ones, and they deserved so much more. Abortion bans unjustly took them from us.

In 2024, the Gender Equity Policy Institute reported that maternal deaths in Texas increased by 56% between 2019 and 2022, compared to an 11% increase nationwide during the same time period. "There's only one explanation for this staggering difference in maternal mortality. All the research points to Texas' abortion ban [S.B. 8, which took effect in September 2021] as the primary driver of this alarming increase," the organization's president said. And, again, abortion bans also increase the risk of suicide, per a 2022 study from the University of Pennsylvania—this is another threat to pregnant people's lives.[2] In 2022, Ohio doctors filed an affidavit challenging the state's then-active abortion ban; they referenced the stories of three women in the state who had recently threatened suicide over being denied abortions. This, of course, is an entirely understandable reaction: Pregnancy, birth, and parenthood can change lives and, if imposed on someone by the state as a punishment, can rob people of their futures.

Prior to *Dobbs*, maternal mortality rates had been steadily increasing for years. By 2017, the maternal mortality rate for young millennial women had more than doubled since the baby-boomer generation. A report put forth by the Center for Reproductive Rights that same year showed states with more restrictions on abortion had higher maternal mortality rates. In 2015, South Carolina's maternal mortality rate spiked by nearly 300%, amid the fallout of increasing restrictions on abortion access.[3] That same year, a third of women in the state reported having no dedicated health care provider. Communities of color suffer from significantly higher maternal mortality than white communities—Black pregnant people are three to four times more likely to die from pregnancy and birth-related causes, in no small part due to medical racism and racialized barriers to access health care. A report published by National Partnership for Women & Families in May 2024 showed 57% of Black women and pregnant-capable people ages 15 to 49 live in states with bans or significant threats to abortion access.[4]

As journalist Susan Rinkunas wrote in 2022, pregnancy is an innate "risk to the lives of women and pregnant people":

> Untreated miscarriages, dangerous deliveries, and other pregnancy-related health problems contribute to a shockingly high maternal mortality rate in the U.S. This mortality rate doesn't even take into account homicide: Pregnant women are more likely to be killed, often at the hands of an intimate partner, than they are to die of health problems in America.

The U.S. maternal mortality rate, as presented to us via state and federal data, is inevitably undercounted. Homicide presents a grave risk to pregnant people—perhaps even more so than health-related complications—but homicides aren't even tracked among pregnancy-related deaths in the U.S.

Suppression of tracking maternal mortality presents a crisis of its own post-*Dobbs*, as the state attempts to not just inflict gendered violence via abortion bans but also to conceal it. In 2024, shortly after ProPublica published reports on Miller and Thurman's abortion ban-induced deaths by consulting with anonymous members of Georgia's maternal mortality committee, the state disbanded the entire committee in retaliation for sharing data with the media. Around the same time, leaders of Texas' maternal mortality committee, appointed by the zealously anti-abortion administration of Governor Greg Abbott, announced they wouldn't analyze maternal mortality data from 2022 to 2023—the first years after the state's sweeping abortion ban took effect.

In 2023, Idaho unceremoniously ended its maternal mortality review committee, before bowing to public pressure and passing a bill to reinstate it the following year. This came around the same time that the state's criminal abortion ban—which offers only an ambiguous exception to save the pregnant person's life, whatever that means, and otherwise threatens doctors with prison—began driving OB-GYNs maternal care providers out of the state in droves. In March 2023, a hospital in a rural region of Idaho was forced to shutter its entire labor and delivery department after an exodus of OB-GYNs who feared that continuing to do their jobs in the state could land them in prison. (Since, several more hospitals in the state have shuttered their maternal care departments.)

Just months earlier, in December 2022, Idaho resident Carmen Broesder documented her 19-day miscarriage in a series of gut-wrenching videos, expressing fear that she would die before anyone helped her due to the state's abortion ban. Despite the excruciating pain and severe blood loss she experienced, Broesder was denied the emergency abortion procedure that would have safely ended her miscarriage and averted further health complications. She told me in the spring of 2023 that she sought the procedure from OB-GYNs in her state twice but was turned away. "A doctor told me 'don't come back until your pain or bleeding is worse,' like I'm dying," Broesder said. She went to another hospital where she says a doctor "looked at me with pity but said 'there's confusion, trepidation regarding the abortion law,'" and he couldn't act yet. Kimra Luna, the co-founder of the organization Idaho Abortion Rights Collective (IARC), told me in March 2023 that Broesder's story was among the most publicly visible, but IARC had heard from and supported numerous callers with similar experiences.

In addition to suppression of maternal mortality and morbidity tracking, since the overturn of *Roe*, anti-abortion state governments have also appointed bad actors to these tracking committees, as we saw in Texas in 2024. For years, Texas has suffered from one of the worst maternal mortality rates in the nation, which only worsened after the state's abortion ban took effect. In May 2024, the state health department then announced one of the 23-member maternal mortality committee's seven new appointees: Dr. Ingrid Skop, a rabidly anti-abortion OB-GYN who testified before Congress in 2021 that child rape victims as young as nine and ten years old could safely carry pregnancies and give birth. Skop's testimony came as part of her arguments for why abortion bans shouldn't include rape exceptions, and ignored how pregnancy at such a young age comes with significant health risks and a substantially greater risk of mortality—all on top of the obvious long-term trauma of being a pregnant, child rape victim. "If she is developed enough to be menstruating and become pregnant and reach sexual maturity, she can safely give birth to a baby," Skop said in 2021. Shortly after Skop was introduced as a new member of the state's maternal mortality committee, she wrote in the *Houston Chronicle*: "For over 30 years, I have advocated for both of my patients, a pregnant woman and her unborn child."

In the summer of 2023, Reverend Dr. Love Holt, an organizer with Abortion Action Missouri and an abortion doula, told Congress that she nearly died earlier that year due to a delay in getting medical help during complications from a medication abortion. Upon learning she was pregnant, she ordered abortion pills, but the first set was stolen, and the replacement pills she ordered didn't arrive until days later. By the time she received the medication, she was past 13 weeks pregnant; abortion pills are most effective before 13 weeks, she noted, but she decided to take the medication anyway. Within minutes, she said, she began intensely bleeding, cramping, and becoming lightheaded, eventually going to her car so she wouldn't "traumatize my children from the sight of seeing me constantly spilling blood." Her children found her in her car unresponsive; she was "rushed off to the ER for severe blood loss," and "nodded in and out of consciousness for several minutes." Holt recounted being taken to the ER of a Catholic hospital and said that "instead of thinking about survival, I thought about not going to jail." She continued, "I told myself, 'Make sure you tell staff that you're having a miscarriage,' but I knew I was having an abortion."

Medication abortion is highly safe, and rarely results in complications.[5] But, as with any medication, if complications arise, people should feel safe immediately seeking medical help. Holt told me in July 2023 that her experience was "a glimpse at the future for hundreds of thousands of people" who will be forced to fear the legal ramifications of getting help to end a pregnancy. "Forcing people to carry unwanted pregnancies drives people into further positions of poverty," she continued. "Poverty gives birth to violence and survival modes that make people unpredictable. They do things that they would normally not do."

A year prior to Holt's remarks before Congress, and just one month before *Dobbs*, she'd shared her story in an op-ed: "Back in 2014, I never would have guessed that one day I would be living in an America that disapproves of my choice to a medical abortion after conceiving amidst an abusive marriage," Holt wrote. She continued:

> I decided to leave my abuser after giving birth to my fourth child while enduring physical and emotional abuse, but he knew that five children would restrict my ability to leave. The decision to leave was tough, but I knew that if I could survive this abuse, I would have an opportunity to raise my current children free from violence . . . I share my story to emphasize the importance of *Roe v. Wade* and the impacts the anticipated Supreme Court decision will have on those most at risk: Black people, people of color, people surviving economic insecurity, trans people, immigrants, youth, people with disabilities and especially those who have been subjected to abuse.

Holt further noted that her state, Missouri, suffered from the third highest rate of domestic violence in the U.S., and that "Black women experience domestic violence at a higher rate than many other groups and are two-and-a-half times more likely to die at the hands of their abusers."

Holt's abortion experiences reflect the reality of dual violence that pregnant people can experience, all exacerbated by abortion bans. Pregnancy endangers victims in abusive relationships, and the threat of health complications during pregnancy endangers their lives, too.

Gun Violence, Domestic Violence, and Abortion Bans

In Oklahoma, which banned abortion after *Dobbs* and has the highest rate of domestic violence in the nation, advocates working in victim services warned that the state's new abortion laws have put victims at greater risk. A forensic nurse administrator at the Tulsa Police Department told *Mother Jones* in 2024 that they've seen some abusers "just keep the patient pregnant so they can't leave." Durrani told me that, among a range of horrific experiences with reproductive coercion that have been reported to the Hotline, one caller said their partner didn't allow her to use contraception, and then threatened to kill her after she became pregnant; another caller became pregnant in a state that banned abortion after her partner sexually assaulted her. Again, in 2023, the Hotline revealed that calls involving acts of reproductive coercion doubled between the summer before *Dobbs* and the summer after.

At the same time the Supreme Court issued the *Dobbs* ruling, it also issued the ruling *New York State Rifle and Pistol Association v. Bruen*, which recognized a constitutional right to carry a handgun in public for self-defense and struck down a New York state restriction on firearms, consequently making them more accessible. The dual timing of these decisions to limit abortion access and potentially expand firearm access to abusers had compounding impacts for pregnant domestic violence victims.

In May 2023, Harold Thompson used a gun to kill his girlfriend Gabriela Gonzalez for having an abortion; he held that gun despite police reports documenting his history of violence toward Gonzalez. Between 2018 and 2022, the number of women who have been shot and killed by an abuser nearly doubled in the state of Texas,[6] which both bans abortion and suffers from endemic gun violence. Firearm-related intimate partner violence situations increased by 47% from 2022 to 2023.[7] "The state has made it easier for a man to obtain a gun to kill his partner than it is for a woman to access abortion care," journalist Alanna Vagianos wrote in 2024. Domestic violence victims are five times more likely to be killed by their abuser if a gun is present.

Lisa Pous, a Texas-based survivor of intimate partner violence, told HuffPost in 2024 that ever since the state's abortion laws took effect, she and other survivors "can't tell the difference anymore between who's harming us," referring to the government and their abusers. "To me, these laws say that my government doesn't care if I die, the same way my partner didn't." Pous also pointed to Texas' S.B. 8 law, which, again, allows people to sue anyone who helps someone have an abortion in the state for at least $10,000: "You can't trust your partner, you can't ask someone for help, your neighbors are now hunting you—it makes the entire world unsafe. How are we supposed to leave [our abusers]? What is the point of leaving?" Pous concluded, "A lot of us really thought we were finding ways out of violence. When the laws changed, we realized . . . we may never make it out."

One attorney representing sexual abuse victims in an abortion-banned state told me in 2024 that she lives in a part of the state where human trafficking of immigrants, particularly minors, is rampant. Pregnancy placed their lives at particular risk thanks to abortion bans, and as did laws that policed speech about abortion and threatened to criminalize adults who helped minors travel out of state for abortion. The attorney, who requested anonymity so her community wouldn't be identified, said these laws made it difficult for her, her colleagues, and abortion funds to know what they could or couldn't advise their clients without the threat of prison. "It was like seeing someone come to you with a really bad cut, and you have a band-aid, but you're not allowed to give it to them."

Sara Ainsworth, senior legal and policy director at the reproductive justice legal organization If/When/How, told me for my reporting in Jezebel that advocates who would otherwise help pregnant victims get the abortion care they need are increasingly struggling to navigate the thorny, constantly changing legal landscape surrounding abortion access, because they "themselves feel targeted by [abortion] laws" like Texas' S.B. 8. Their work has never been easy, Ainsworth said, but now, "between fears for their own [legal] safety, or confusion about how these very new, untested laws are going to be enforced," it's only gotten harder—and victims pay the price.

At the end of 2024, Texas Public Radio reported that domestic violence shelters across the state were facing surges of pregnant victims and victims with newborns ever since Texas' total abortion ban took effect.[8] Verónica Cruz Sánchez, a Mexican activist who's sent hundreds of packs of medication abortion across the border since 2022, told the outlet of at least one case of a domestic violence victim she worked with who had to give birth because her abusive partner would kill her if abortion pills she'd ordered arrived to their home. Family Violence Prevention Services, the largest domestic violence shelter in Texas' Bexar County, said they've seen a 12% increase since 2022 in clients who are pregnant or have newborns. Three other shelters reported similar data.

In *Survivor Injustice*, I looked at each state's reported domestic violence rate and found that nearly every state that had imposed some form of abortion ban in 2019 or 2020 also had a higher domestic violence rate than the national average. These states included Georgia, Kentucky, Louisiana, Mississippi, Ohio, Missouri, North Dakota, South Dakota, Idaho, Arkansas, Utah,

Montana, Tennessee, Alabama, Oklahoma, Iowa, Texas, and Wyoming. Of these 18 states, 15 have rates of domestic abuse that are higher than the national average, which stands at about 33% of women and 25% of men, per the National Domestic Violence Hotline's 2019 data.

Anti-abortion laws in these states are often part of an over-arching state-wide policy landscape that inflicts disparate harm on victims and survivors. Notably, out of these aforementioned states, Alabama, Iowa, Oklahoma, Mississippi, Kentucky, Ohio, South Dakota, and Wyoming also have laws that don't allow for a spouse to be convicted of "raping a partner who was unconscious, drugged, or otherwise incapacitated," as well as laws that exclude spousal rape from the criminalization of "statutory rape and/or sexual contact between people with a supervisory relationship," *Mother Jones* reported.[9] In 2019, the same year Louisiana's governor signed a six-week abortion ban (which couldn't take effect until *Dobbs* in 2022), its district attorneys unanimously blocked a bill that would have protected sexual violence victims from being jailed to coerce testimony against their abusers.

If, as Domestic Shelters' Rita Smith pointed out, abortion bans are exposing "a cultural shift in what the value of women's lives is," they aren't alone in this—an entire political system is colluding with these laws to enact unspeakable violence on pregnant people, particularly pregnant abuse victims.

Medical Violence and Abortion Bans

In the summer of 2024, a question of the "value of women's lives" lay at the heart of a Supreme Court case, *Moyle v. United States*, in which Idaho argued its abortion ban took precedence over EMTALA (the Emergency Medical Treatment and Labor

Act), a federal law establishing a right for all people to receive emergency care, including abortion.

Since 1986, EMTALA has required hospitals to provide stabilizing health care to patients, including those experiencing pregnancy-related complications, superseding individual state laws. In some cases, abortion is necessary to save a pregnant person's life or help them reach a stable condition, but Idaho's ban as it's written allows abortion only if the pregnant person is imminently dying. In *Moyle*, the court ruled that, for the time being, doctors in Idaho could adhere to EMTALA without facing prosecution—but ultimately handed the case back down to a lower court, preserving the matter in a sort of legal limbo. Months later, in December that year, attorneys for Idaho argued in state court that even if pregnancy complications threaten to cost someone a limb, hospitals should still deny them emergency abortion care.

Idaho's abortion ban and similar laws in other states all but ask providers to violate EMTALA and all basic medical ethics, and engage in what an amicus brief filed by Democracy Forward in March 2024 characterized as "expectant management"—or, the "wait and see approach"—and withhold "treatment necessary to protect their patient's health and [wait] to perform a clinically indicated abortion until it becomes necessary to prevent death."

The arguments put forth in *Moyle* also carried chilling implications for fetal personhood, as Idaho argued that an embryo or unborn fetus is a "patient" whose rights should precede the pregnant person's—and Justices Samuel Alito and Neil Gorsuch concurred during oral arguments. Texas' attorney general, Ken Paxton, made this same argument when the state successfully sued the Biden administration in 2022, claiming Texas shouldn't have to adhere to Biden's guidance that hospitals follow EMTALA and offer emergency abortions when necessary: "EMTALA contemplates that an emergency medical condition is one that threatens the life of the unborn child," Paxton's legal complaint said. Under this interpretation, patients aren't living pregnant people—only fetuses are.

Just months before the *Moyle* ruling, in February 2024, the Alabama Supreme Court ruled frozen embryos are unborn "extrauterine children," forcing fertility clinics across the state to pause IVF services until the legislature passed bipartisan legislation that explicitly protected IVF. Of course, even before this appraisal by the Alabama court, people have long faced criminal charges for miscarriages, alleged self-managed abortions, or other behavior deemed to "endanger" their "child," or rather, their fetus. In Pregnancy Justice's amicus brief for *Moyle*, the organization argued that Idaho purposely misinterpreted EMTALA to make a case for fetal personhood and devalue pregnant people's lives:

> Idaho latches onto EMTALA's references to "unborn child" . . . and claims that Congress must have guaranteed an EMTALA right to two patients equally: the pregnant woman and the fetus she carries . . . Nothing in EMTALA's plain language supports Idaho's radical attempt to re-write federal law.

Abortion itself is highly safe—you're 14 times more likely to die in childbirth than having an abortion.[10] Meanwhile, pregnancy itself is an innately dangerous experience, sometimes due to preexisting health conditions or pregnancy complications, and in other cases, due to domestic violence; for those with certain chronic conditions, the risk is even greater, and abortion bans can either kill or drastically shorten their life spans and long-term health.

Nisha Verma, an OB-GYN in Georgia and a fellow with Physicians for Reproductive Health, said in 2022 that she once served a patient who was diagnosed with a rare cancer while pregnant.[11] The patient, who wanted to be pregnant, ultimately needed to have an abortion to begin chemotherapy and try to maximize her chance of survival: "If that patient couldn't get her chemotherapy because she's forced to continue her pregnancy, she's not going to die in that moment, but she probably will die much sooner. Maybe significantly sooner, decades sooner," Verma said. In the fall of 2022, Ohio doctors filed a brief as part of a legal challenge against the state's abortion ban detailing the stories of not just multiple underage rape victims who were forced to travel out of state for abortions, but two pregnant women who had cancer and couldn't immediately begin chemotherapy because they couldn't get abortions in the state. And in 2024, ANSIRH (Advancing New Standards in Reproductive Health), of the University of California, San Francisco, published a study compiling dozens of physician anecdotes about the impact of abortion bans on their ability to provide standard medical care. In one case, a woman who learned she was pregnant after being diagnosed with breast cancer was told she couldn't start chemotherapy until she had an abortion—but abortion was banned in her state. At that point, she was six weeks pregnant; it took her seven additional weeks to obtain an abortion in a nearby state. In a similar case, doctors canceled a liver transplant for a patient in a state that banned abortion because they discovered she was pregnant. The study, collected from September 2022 to August 2024, contains over 85 stories like these.

"For some people [abortion] is a preventive measure to help them maintain their health, and for some people it is acute health care where someone is at an immediate or near-immediate risk," Verma said. "Abortion is absolutely lifesaving."

Violence as a Tool of the Anti-Abortion Movement

Denial of health care is innately violent. Forced pregnancy is a danger to domestic violence victims, as well as people suffering from emergency medical conditions. This—state violence, psychic violence, physical violence—plays a central role in the anti-abortion movement, which, for decades, has relied on terror attacks, arson, assault, vandalism, harassment, even murder, against abortion providers, staff, and volunteers. All of this is inextricably connected to the violence of anti-abortion policies. Anti-abortion violence has been steadily on the rise for years: In May 2023, the National Abortion Federation (NAF) reported that, from 2021 to 2022, there was a 229% increase in stalking, 231% increase in burglaries, and 100% increase in clinic arsons (from two cases in 2021 to four in 2022) at abortion clinics across the country. As clinics continue to shutter due to state abortion bans, those that remain in service have consequently become even more vulnerable to anti-abortion harassment and threats.

In journalist Lauren Rankin's book *Bodies On the Line: At the Frontlines of the Fight to Protect Abortion in America*, published just weeks before *Dobbs* in 2022, Rankin tells the stories of several people who lost family members and loved ones who were abortion providers to terrorism perpetrated by anti-abortion activists. Dandy Barrett's father James had been volunteering as an abortion clinic escort—someone who supports and accompanies patients into clinics, often through a gauntlet of harassing protesters—for just over a year, in the wake of the 1993 political assassination of Florida abortion provider Dr. David Gunn. One summer morning in 1994, Dandy received a call that changed her life: Her father had been shot and killed while driving into his clinic's parking lot.

This wasn't an isolated incident. Clinic violence doesn't happen in a vacuum; anti-abortion leaders and politicians are constantly fanning the flames for it by equating abortion with murder.

Yet, despite the severity and frequency of physical violence deployed by anti-abortion protesters, their tactics and protests are rarely taken seriously by local law enforcement. Rankin's *Bodies On the Line* details numerous cases of police shrugging off the threat posed by anti-abortion protesters, being openly supportive of protesters, or victim-blaming escorts and providers. "They're told [by police], 'this is what you signed up for,' as a provider or volunteer," Rankin told me in 2022. For some escorts and clinic staff, calling police isn't even an option, as police presence is inherently "unsafe for a lot of people of color, particularly undocumented immigrants," and "can place Black people's lives at risk," she said.

In May 2024, a federal judge sentenced anti-abortion activist Lauren Handy—who stole five aborted fetuses from an abortion clinic in 2022—to almost five years in prison for invading a Washington, D.C., clinic in 2020, following her conviction under the Freedom of Access to Clinic Entrances (FACE) Act in August 2023. (The FACE Act was enacted in the 1990s to prohibit anti-abortion protesters from blocking entry to abortion clinics, following years of extreme and highly visible anti-abortion violence and obstruction.) Handy's eight co-defendants, who joined her in illegally invading and blockading the D.C. clinic by chaining themselves together to the premises, received the same sentence. One of her co-defendants had assaulted a clinic nurse who then sprained her ankle. Another knocked a woman experiencing labor pains to the floor, then physically blocked her from entering the clinic. Just one month before Handy's sentencing, in California, a former U.S. Marine and neo-Nazi who firebombed a Planned Parenthood clinic in 2022 was sentenced to nine years in federal prison.

In the spring of 2023, in Illinois, an independent abortion clinic under construction in Danville was attacked by a 73-year-old man who repeatedly drove his car into the walls of the building structure, destroying most of the front lobby and the back of the clinic site. According to police, the man planned to set the facility on fire before being apprehended. The building was meant to house Affirmative Care Solutions, a sister clinic to Indiana's Clinic for Women. Within days, Abortion Care Network, an organization of independent clinics including Affirmative Care Solutions, shared that the under-construction clinic faced yet another attack from a different anti-abortion vandal just two weeks after the first. The clinic needed "to hire security guards, rebuild destroyed walls and the lobby, and fortify and refurbish the entire structure." The attacks came as Illinois faced the second-highest increase in abortions in any state since the Supreme Court overturned *Roe*.[12] As recently as the beginning of 2025, the Danville clinic still hadn't opened yet due to the destruction.

As more people than ever have come to rely on Illinois-based abortion providers for care, the targeted violence that clinics in the state face has surged, too. And the consecutive attacks on the Danville-based, under-construction clinic also came at a time of mounting hostility toward abortion access in the community, as Danville city council members voted to instate a ban on mailing abortion pills. Elsewhere in Illinois, abortion providers reported a rise in anti-abortion violence, including the January 2023 fire-bombing of a Planned Parenthood clinic in the city of Peoria.

Between 2019 and 2020, despite the COVID pandemic, abortion providers across the country reported an increase in "vandalism, assault and battery, death threats/threats of harm, stalking, and hoax devices/suspicious packages," according to a December 2021 report by the National Abortion Federation. Providers reported a 125% increase in assaults and altercations instigated by anti-abortion protesters, and in that same time period, death threats and threats of harm to clinic staff more than doubled.

"We expected an escalation in anti-abortion activities in 2020 and 2021 due to the political climate, the election, and the increase in hate incidents throughout the country," Melissa Fowler, chief program officer of NAF, told me back in 2021. Fowler also raised that "some of the people at the January 6, 2021 [Capitol] insurrection are the same people who have been targeting abortion providers and protesting at clinics in their communities."

"The people who threaten clinic workers and harass individuals seeking abortion care are often the same people who participate in other violent and extremist activities that are rooted in racism, white supremacy, and misogyny, and are deeply harmful," she said.

Anti-abortion leaders and lawmakers have long tried to distance themselves from more overt anti-abortion violence against providers and advocates, as we saw in the aftermath of the 2015 mass shooting at a Planned Parenthood clinic in Colorado by a man who said he "killed three and saved 3,000 babies." Yet, however "pro-life" these individuals may claim to be, when they equate a health service and ending an unwanted pregnancy to killing a baby, they're inevitably inviting violence against people who provide and have abortions—and they know it. On the state-level, over the last decade, several states including Oklahoma, Georgia, Texas, and Alabama have introduced bills that would make abortion a felony punishable by the death penalty; the spring of 2023 saw a wave of similar such bills in state legislatures. In 2024, the Texas Republican party called for abortion to be recognized as homicide under the state criminal code—that's a crime punishable with the death penalty. In the first two weeks of 2025, four state legislatures—in Oklahoma, South Carolina, North Dakota, and Indiana—introduced bills that would similarly recognize abortion as homicide, and thus, in three of those four states, potentially threaten abortion patients with the death penalty.

When abortion providers and their supporters are framed as baby killers, this incites retaliation in kind.

Further, the state affords no real protections to abortion patients, providers, and advocates. In the summer of 2022, shortly after *Dobbs*, FBI Director Christopher Wray testified before the Senate that his bureau had opened "a number" of investigations into abortion-related violent crime incidents from both abortion opponents and abortion rights supporters, which he said had surged since *Dobbs*. Wray claimed there had been "a general intensification of violence across the issue," echoing similar warnings issued by the Department of Homeland Security months earlier. Wray and DHS played into a false equivalence of violence allegedly perpetrated by abortion rights advocates and violence from the anti-abortion movement. Government panics about violence from abortion rights activists aren't new: In 2019, journalist Anna Merlan reported on a briefing that the FBI sent to law enforcement agencies warning of the threat of "pro-abortion extremists." Recall that between that year and 2020, reported physical violence targeting abortion providers surged by 125%. It seems no matter what anti-abortion activists do—assassinate abortion providers, run online registries doxxing clinic staff and volunteers, even conspire to kidnap abortion providers' children,[13] or, of course, wield the law to violently compel unwanted pregnancy and birth—abortion advocates and patients will always be the ones on law enforcement's radar. In 2022, the city of Louisville, Kentucky, paid a police officer $75,000 in settlement fees after the officer was suspended for protesting outside a local abortion clinic armed and in uniform. In effect, he was paid by the state to harass and intimidate abortion providers and patients. On top of all of this, abortion providers are being threatened with years of prison for offering a health service, while pregnant people routinely face state surveillance and criminal charges for pregnancy-related decisions and outcomes, including abortion.

Violence is a central piece of the anti-abortion movement's strategy—violence inflicted on patients who suffer from medical emergencies, domestic violence exacerbated by abortion bans, horrific threats on the lives of abortion providers. Anti-abortion lawmakers have long insisted their movement doesn't punish abortion patients. But to ban abortion *is* to punish patients, to endanger their lives, to potentially kill them—if not immediately, then over time. Fundamentally, theirs is an ideology of violence.

Chapter 3

How Abusers Weaponize Pregnancy in the Legal System

In March 2023, within months of *Dobbs*, we faced a terrifying first: A Texas man named Marcus Silva, aided by the notoriously underhanded anti-abortion attorney Jonathan Mitchell, filed a "wrongful death" lawsuit against three women claiming they helped his ex-wife have an abortion in July 2022 "without [his] knowledge or consent." The suit argued abortion is murder; it didn't directly invoke Texas' abortion laws, but it reflects the model of Texas' S.B. 8, which allows people to sue anyone who allegedly helped someone have an abortion for at least $10,000. Silva and Mitchell sought $1 million in damages.

Silva produced text messages and photos he obtained by going through his ex's phone and purse; the photos and messages, which he shared with police, suggested one of his ex-wife's three friends obtained medication abortion for her to self-manage her abortion at home.

Weeks after Silva filed the suit, two of the women, Jackie Noyola and Amy Carpenter, counter-sued Silva. Their suit called Silva a "serial emotional abuser" who "had spent years verbally attacking [his then-wife], seeking to manipulate and control" her. Silva "did not file this lawsuit because he is interested in 'protecting life.' Instead, he wanted to control a life, [his ex's]," the women's suit said. Attorneys for Silva's ex-wife later said in an October 2023 court filing that his suit was just "the latest abusive tactic in a long line of steps he has taken to harass and control" her, alleging he'd previously threatened to post a video of them having sex on Pornhub and threatened her with years-long litigation harassment if she didn't continue a sexual relationship with him after the divorce, which was finalized in February 2023. In the countersuit, the women also point to how Silva told police he found a phone number for an abortion clinic hotline in his ex-wife's purse, and also found the abortion pills— but instead of trying to stop her, he waited months and filed his lawsuit simply to punish her:

> Rather than talking with [his ex-wife] about what he found or disposing of the pill, Silva took photos of the texts and surreptitiously put the pill back. He wasn't interested in stopping her from terminating a possible pregnancy. Instead, he wanted to obtain evidence he could use against her if she refused to stay under his control, which is precisely what he tried to do.

The women's countersuit also includes texts between Silva's ex-wife and her friends in which she recounts how he threatened to have her put in jail for having an abortion, if "I don't give him my 'mind, body and soul' until the end of the divorce, which he's going to drag out," she wrote.

> So now that's being held over my head and I feel stuck because I'm a fucking idiot . . . If I try to leave I think he's going to use that against me . . . If I don't do what he wants I know he will do that shit. He's shown me messages even with his dad egging him on to do it.

Mitchell, Silva's lawyer, is the architect behind some of the most convoluted and dangerous abortion legislation in the nation—including Texas' S.B. 8. Within a year of Silva's lawsuit, Mitchell represented at least two more men in taking legal action regarding their ex-partners' alleged abortions: In March 2024, Mitchell helped another Texas man file a legal complaint to try to depose his ex-partner for allegedly traveling out of state for abortion. The petition claimed the alleged abortion amounted to wrongful death under Texas state law and additionally cited S.B. 8. Per the petition, the man's intent was to identify who helped his ex-partner have an abortion, identify her abortion provider, and sue all of them. In the legal petition, Mitchell refers to the alleged out-of-state abortion in question as "murder" 23 times. An attorney for the woman, Molly Duane of the Center for Reproductive Rights, told me at the time that the man had been emotionally abusive to her client, and that Mitchell was "behind multiple attempts by hostile, and in some cases abusive, ex-boyfriends or ex-husbands, to take legal action against women who allegedly obtained abortions." She explained, "This is all the inevitable outcome of *Roe* being overturned—IVF threats, wrongful death suits, women being punished, all of it."[1]

In May 2024, the *Texas Tribune* reported that Mitchell had filed nine such legal petitions targeting people over abortions, primarily against abortion providers and advocates. But in at least one case other than those already mentioned, at an unspecified time, Mitchell began representing another Texas man attempting to sue his ex-partner for an abortion. In a filing obtained by the *Tribune*, that woman's lawyers said that enabling Mitchell's strategy of intimidation and harassment would endanger women across the state. Under the guise of collecting information for a potential lawsuit, petitioners like Mitchell "would be entitled to depose and seek documents from any woman who is not now pregnant, but was rumored to be at some time." The attorneys argued that "any woman who has a miscarriage could be subject to a forced interrogation," and "any scorned lover could harass or intimidate their ex . . . for simply receiving a false-positive pregnancy test."[2]

Contrary to Mitchell's claims used to harass these women, traveling out of state for abortion is legal—no matter what misinformation, intimidation, or legal gymnastics anti-abortion activists like Mitchell try to push, weaponizing the orchestrated complexity of abortion laws to target and control pregnant people and particularly pregnant abuse victims.

Confusion about abortion laws (which are, indeed, very confusing) has become a uniquely terrifying tool at the disposal of abusive partners. Recall that the National Domestic Violence Hotline published a survey on reproductive coercion showing that since *Dobbs*, 5% of over 3,000 survey respondents (close to 200 people) said abusive partners threatened to report them to police or other authorities for considering having an abortion. Another 5% said abusive partners threatened to sue or take them to court if they sought abortion.

At the same time as Mitchell's legal actions on behalf of abusive men, several states moved to pass legislation to criminalize the act of helping minors travel out of state for abortion care without parental consent, calling this "abortion trafficking." Some anti-abortion activists have even called for anti-trafficking laws to apply to fetuses, when someone travels out of state for abortion. Tennessee enacted an "abortion trafficking" law in the summer of 2024, threatening those in violation with a Class A misdemeanor, which carries up to a one-year prison sentence. Legal experts warned that a law like this yields disparate harm for underage sexual abuse victims or minors who may not have trusted parents or guardians, or who might live in abusive homes. Tennessee's law could specifically be wielded as a tool for abusers, Jessica Goldberg, youth access counsel at If/When/How, told me for my reporting in 2024: "We know that bans on abortion support have been weaponized by abusers to further abuse and to harass their victims or their victims' loved ones through abusive litigation and campaigns of terror. This opens the door for that to happen." Due to the overwhelming popularity of abortion rights, anti-abortion activists have relied on convoluted, fearmongering tactics, for example, framing abortion and reproductive health as a "parental rights" issue. In 2024, a circuit court in Texas ruled that minors seeking birth control needed parental consent to obtain it; one judge wrote that, like the plaintiff suing to stop his daughters from getting birth control, he wanted to stop his own daughter from having premarital sex, and access to birth control would—God forbid—grant her bodily autonomy. Legal attacks on reproductive care always target minors first but pave the way for all our rights to be dismantled soon after.

So-called "abortion trafficking" policies have already expanded in scope beyond minors. In 2023 and 2024, a rash of counties across Texas enacted abortion travel bans, which outlaw use of roads within the county if individuals are traveling for abortion care as a means to stop "abortion trafficking." The county ordinances, enforced by threat of costly lawsuits, apply to abortion seekers of all ages. Farah Diaz-Tello, senior legal counsel at If/When/How, told me even if these county bans aren't really enforceable in practice, they still fulfill their purpose of "chaos and confusion." She explained, "If not even trained lawyers can parse this, how are people who are just trying to figure out what their options are, how they can support their loved ones, supposed to get any of this?"

In the months leading up to *Dobbs*, several states followed Texas' lead in adopting bounty hunter-style, civilly enforced abortion bans like S.B. 8. These laws created the innate potential for rapists and abusers to use the legal system to harass their victims and profit off their pregnancies. In March 2022, Slate's Dahlia Lithwick and Mark Joseph Stern wrote that such bans invite "Lyft drivers, high school counselors, and neighbors" to police someone's pregnancy. Idaho's version of S.B. 8, introduced in the spring of 2022, carried an extra dimension of terror, allowing the family members of the "father" of the fetus to also sue accessories to an abortion for damages.

Texas' S.B. 8 doesn't—nor do the state's other abortion bans— include rape exceptions. Rape-induced pregnancies aren't uncommon: Again, research from 2024 estimated between June 2022 and January 2024, over 500,000 rapes in abortion-banned states "were associated with 64,565 pregnancies." Of these nearly 65,000 rape-induced pregnancies, "58,979 (91%) [were] in states with no [rape] exception," with 26,313 (45%) in Texas. When Texas Gov. Greg Abbott was challenged by reporters about S.B. 8's lack of a rape exception in 2021, he shrugged this off as a non-issue—in his own words, he would simply "eliminate rape." Clearly, as the January 2024 research showed, he didn't. Just over three years after his "eliminate rape" line, Abbott proudly erected a host of billboards along the border in December 2024, warning any immigrants who crossed that they or their children will inevitably be raped. Unsurprisingly, Abbott—the same man who wants rape victims in his state to carry their rapists' babies—also sees widespread sexual violence against immigrants as nothing more than a political opportunity.[3]

In October 2024, just days before Silva's suit went to trial, he dropped the case. Noyola and Carpenter told me at the time that over the last 19 months, they'd witnessed how abortion bans and the legal system empower abusers and disempower victims: "It's insane to us the state of Texas is just colluding with abusers by banning abortions, honestly promoting bounty hunting laws," Noyola said. "That's what lawsuits like this are meant to do—scare you." Carpenter determined that Texas' abortion laws are meant to help "someone like him [Silva]—we all know the type, right?—destroy a victim's support system in this big, bold way." For months, both women had to speak to each other and one of their closest friends through attorneys, fearing legal repercussions.

"[Silva's lawsuit] was meant to send a message, to have a chilling effect," Diaz-Tello told me in October 2024. "Isolation is a common tactic of abusers—and that's what the state is doing." Since *Dobbs*, we've seen a range of tactics to not just enforce state abortion bans but coerce and entrap people under these laws. Duane told me that this mirrors the actions of abusive partners who try to similarly entrap their victims: "It's all about fear, chaos, cruelty in the extreme."

In November 2024, within days of Donald Trump winning reelection, anti-abortion organizations detailed new strategies to further erode reproductive rights. Texas Right to Life, the most powerful anti-abortion organization in the state, announced a recruitment call for abusive men seeking to sue ex-partners for having abortions. They rolled out advertising campaigns for this venture on Facebook and Twitter/X in January 2025.

The attorney general of Texas reportedly launched his own underground recruitment operation around the same time, finding a man willing to report his partner's abortion to the state, which gave way to a lawsuit against a New York doctor in December 2024; the lawsuit threatens to challenge laws in pro-choice states that allow doctors to legally send abortion pills to residents of abortion-banned states. As anti-abortion activists and government officials try to crack down on abortion pills from out-of-state and pro-choice websites, they need plaintiffs; they're recruiting abusive partners specifically for that purpose. Even if these partners weren't abusive before, attempting to sue someone over their abortion—an excruciatingly invasive, torturous process that could expose someone to state surveillance, criminalization, and public humiliation—is fundamentally abusive on its own. Texas Right to Life told the Washington Post in January 2025 that their "strategy" is "to tell dads that if you're the father of a child victim of an abortion, you have legal rights, there may be a way to hold these people accountable." He continued, "Historically, fathers didn't have legal standing. They were shut out of the whole thing, because [the law said], 'It's a woman's right to choose.'" God forbid!

"Abusers have turned to our legal systems to deny their victims bodily autonomy and further harass them for probably as long as our legal system has existed," Diaz-Tello explained to me. She wasn't "surprised anti-abortion advocates are capitalizing on abusers' misuse of the legal system to further their campaign of fear and terror against abortion seekers." Since *Dobbs*, she said, survivors have been "forced to weigh the risks of their abusive relationships against their access to abortion," and "walk the line of isolation and safety to get the abortion they need, all while trying to minimiz(e) their risks of criminalization and punishment by their abuser and the state."

The legal system has long accorded abusers their pick of avenues to silence or terrorize their victims. Pregnancy only compounds their power: Consider the alarming number of states that prohibit courts from finalizing a divorce during pregnancy, potentially resulting in the pregnancy binding someone to an abusive partner.

Being forced into the legal system can come with significant financial ramifications for victims. Of the $3.1 trillion in lifetime economic costs of experiencing rape, according to the National Sexual Violence Resource Center, $234 billion are siphoned into legal fees. Idaho's abortion bounty hunter law from 2022 offered at least $20,000. As the bill was introduced, one Idaho lawmaker on the state House floor asked, "If I am raped and choose to have an abortion and my rapist has 10 siblings, is there anything to preclude all of them and their spouses from bringing a lawsuit for $20,000 each?"

"No," she was told.

A Legal System That Crushes Survivors

The legal system presents such a danger to pregnant survivors because it already presents a danger to survivors, broadly. Sexual violence is vastly underreported to law enforcement, in no small part because officers of law enforcement are frequently perpetrators of sexual violence themselves. Fewer than 1% of rapes lead to convictions,[4] while about 90% of incarcerated women—a majority of whom are women of color—are survivors.[5] It's unsurprising, then, that while accused men are often unsparing in their pursuit of all legal actions they can take to silence or retaliate against victims who come forward, again, most survivors don't report their assaults to authorities at all. It's often victims who are punished or threatened with punishment by the state: One 2020 survey found 24% of women who have called the police to report intimate partner violence say *they* were consequently arrested or threatened with arrest.[6]

In the summer of 2020, amid a nationwide uprising for racial justice, 50 anti-sexual violence organizations signed the "Moment of Truth" letter highlighting the harms of police and prisons on victims of abuse and calling for divestment from the carceral system. Soon after sharing the letter, some of the groups who co-signed it, including local shelters and community anti-violence programs, lost public funding,[7] while others said police departments stopped referring victims to their services.[8]

Race and class play an indelible role in how police and the legal system writ large treat victims. Take, for example, the political and cultural impact of laws like the Violence Against Women Act, and the exclusionary, racialized activism that led to its passage in the 1990s. Prior to VAWA, domestic violence was widely accepted, normalized, and shrugged off as a private matter, exclusively discussed in underground, feminist consciousness-raising circles.[9] Advocacy on behalf of gender-based violence victims began to draw mainstream support amid the tough-on-crime era in the 1980s and 1990s, when awareness campaigns on the issue conflated it with "stranger-danger" violence in the streets. Of course, most gender-based violence is carried out by intimate partners or someone the victim knows, and often takes place at home or otherwise in private. As public awareness and protest of gender-based violence grew, some of the movement's most visible activists ceded its more radical demands to gain wider public support, resulting in collusion with law enforcement and the carceral features of laws like VAWA.

Eventually, VAWA was introduced as part of then-Sen. Joe Biden's 1994 crime bill. Among a range of problems with the law which, in some ways, put victims at greater risk, VAWA allocates most of its funding to police departments to respond to domestic violence, despite their long histories of disbelieving, mistreating, and retraumatizing survivors. VAWA requires that an arrest be made when someone calls the police to report experiencing domestic violence, and can result in victims themselves being criminalized and arrested, sometimes, if police officers deem them the primary aggressor, and other times, to compel them to testify against their abuser if they're afraid to cooperate with law enforcement.

Two different studies from the 1990s show 40% of surveyed police officers self-reporting their own acts of domestic violence.[10] At the same time, police have a documented, persistent history of willfully refusing to believe victims: A 2014 study showed most surveyed officers say they believe most rape reports are false.[11] In reality, the small percentage of reported rapes that are labeled false is likely a significant over-count: A 1996 report compiling police data indicating 8% of rapes are falsely reported is a result of the FBI marking rapes and sexual assaults that didn't involve a weapon, or were reported by people with a prior relationship to their assailants (which is most assaults), as "false reports," Amia Srinivasan found in researching her 2021 book *The Right to Sex*. And when false accusations and reports do happen, they overwhelmingly involve district attorneys or police officers pressuring victims to identify a certain man as their rapist or attacker, in order to close a case and inflate their safety records. Put simply, so-called "false reports" happen, but they aren't coming from the stereotypical, vengeful, lying woman invented by our rabidly anti-feminist cultural imagination.

Courtrooms are hardly friendlier to survivors than police stations are. Survivors are routinely disbelieved and punished for their own testimonies about the gender-based violence to which they've been subjected. In 2022, the civil trial presiding over whether actress Amber Heard defamed her ex-husband, Johnny Depp, by writing an op-ed about surviving domestic violence, offered a chilling glimpse into the legal system's (and general public's) cruelty, as Heard, herself, was portrayed by Depp's legal team as abusive for responding to and fighting back against his abuse. To sexual violence researcher Dr. Nicole Bedera, this particularly high-profile case embodied the everyday abuse tactic known as DARVO (deny, attack, reverse victim and offender): "It's about bringing up things the victim has done to suggest the victim is not a perfect victim, they're not a deserving victim, they're not a good victim," she told me. Sometimes, abusers and their legal representation "deny the abuse happened, and sometimes they just deny that it was wrong, because it was actually 'self-defense'" against their victim. In any case, the message is clear: Victims who don't sufficiently adhere to patriarchal, fundamentally white supremacist ideals of innocence, victims who fight back, victims who, in other words, are "imperfect," aren't credible. Meanwhile, victims who *don't* respond to their abuse, or don't sufficiently try to escape it, aren't credible victims either in our culture and our legal system—why didn't they just leave?

College campuses are often sites of even harsher administrative cruelty toward survivors, weaponizing the worst and most prejudiced aspects of the legal system. Through observation at one large public university's Title IX office between 2018 and 2019, and 76 interviews with Title IX administrators and students at the unnamed university, Bedera found that in most cases, Title IX administrators determined the trauma that victims incurred was either too severe for the university to even try to remedy, or that the women were "hysterical." Sometimes administrators determined that neither party was lying when they had different perspectives on how a sexual encounter had transpired, with women saying they were harmed and men recounting a consensual encounter. But in such cases, men's proclamations of innocence were valued above women saying they felt violated. An attitude that assailants are unfairly punished for engaging in typical "boys will be boys" behavior also prevailed. "There's this myth that men's lives are ruined when they're accused of sexual violence—it isn't just untrue, it becomes the justification for giving them benefits, for giving them more power and privilege as the result of the sexual violence they commit, to compensate for that notion," Bedera told me.

An estimated 34% of campus sexual assault survivors are forced to drop out of their schools, according to one study. Those who report their assaults can even face costly defamation suits from the men they report. In one case uncovered by the campus survivor justice organization Know Your IX, one student's troubles had only just begun when her assailant was expelled: He then launched a "four-year smear campaign" against her, researcher Sage Carson told me in 2022, including a defamation suit that followed her for the rest of her college career. Through the lawsuit, he was able to "access her medical records, school records, even her sexual history." His retaliation eventually forced the student to transfer schools, delay her graduation, and spend over $100,000 trying to protect herself from his attacks. Even when the survivor "won" her Title IX case, she still lost. In many ways, this is what the legal system looks like for survivors.

This is the legal system that now, in some states, presides over whether a rape victim's family owes their rapist thousands of dollars for helping them have an abortion. This is the legal system that determines whether people who helped a domestic violence victim access abortion care to exit an abusive relationship owe her abuser $1 million in damages.

This is the same legal system that mothers who are impregnated by rape have long contended with. We know rape-induced pregnancies in states that have banned abortion are not rare. According to the Centers for Disease Control and Prevention, almost three million women in the U.S. have become pregnant from rape. Those survivors who are unable to access abortion for a rape-induced pregnancy, or may choose to move forward with their pregnancy, could find themselves embroiled in contentious, retraumatizing custody battles with their rapists for years, in an especially cruel form of state violence.

We're already seeing this.

Rapists' Parental Rights Wars

Years before *Dobbs*, a Florida woman named Analyn Megison found herself fighting her rapist in court to keep custody of her five-year-old daughter in 2008. Over the course of the years-long legal battle, Megison told me she was frequently "retraumatized" by being forced to see her rapist in court from 2008 until 2012, when a judge finally denied the man's petition and awarded her sole custody of her young daughter. But her legal woes didn't end there: Years later, a different judge would cite Megison's continued activism to stop rapists from claiming parental rights to their victims' children as justification for granting custody of her oldest son to her abusive ex-husband. Megison told me that this judge said her work would cause her young son to "think negatively about fatherhood." To this day, Megison, who now resides in Arizona, continues to make child support payments to a man who she says once beat her so severely while she was pregnant that she miscarried. When she called the police to report him at the time, Megison told me, they "didn't take the report because they said my husband and me 'were one flesh, you can't beat yourself.'"

The thorny legal territory surrounding rapists' parental rights presents a horrific, years-long—if not endless—avenue through which pregnancy is weaponized as a means for rapists and abusers to exert long-term control and violence over their victims. Megison's experiences showed that there were zero legal protections in place for people like her whose rapists had not been criminally convicted. This motivated her to advocate for legislation to shift the burden of proof required by a mother who accuses her child's father of rape from the "beyond a reasonable doubt" standard applied in criminal cases, to the "clear and convincing evidence" standard used in civil cases, amid contentious custody battles. A bill changing this standard passed out of Florida's legislature in 2013; the federal Rape Survivor Child Custody Act passed in 2015. As of 2024, 32 other states now use the "clear and convincing evidence" legal standard that Megison says helped her win her custody case. Still, this means nearly half of all states continue to require criminal convictions for rapists' parental rights to be automatically terminated.

In the summer of 2022, within days of *Dobbs*, one Louisiana woman who said she had been impregnated by her rapist as a teenager 16 years earlier—when she was 16 and he was 30—briefly lost custody of her child to her rapist. A state judge had granted full custody of Crysta Abelseth's teen daughter to John Barnes, the man Abelseth identified as her rapist, and even required her to pay him child support. This outcome arose solely because Barnes alleged that Abelseth had given her teenage daughter a cell phone. Speaking to local media at the time, Abelseth recounted being mistreated by and turned away from the legal system for years, all while facing near-constant threats from Barnes, who sought to intimidate her to not come forward by citing his "connections in the justice system."

After Abelseth filed criminal charges against Barnes in 2015, right after she learned about an exception to the statute of limitations for child sex crimes, she says nothing happened in the subsequent seven years: "It was never assigned to a detective, and nothing was ever investigated." Court records about Barnes,

Abelseth, and her charges against him were "mysteriously under seal," per the local news outlet that investigated her case.

The same year that Abelseth shared her story, I interviewed an Arizona woman named Darcy Benoit, whose rapist sued for custody of the child she had conceived in 2011. The man was initially granted joint custody. For years, Benoit was forced to co-parent in some capacity with her rapist, and remains forced to respond to his varying legal petitions to this day. A bleak 2017 study[12] found that when mothers allege domestic violence in custody cases, fathers win custody 73% of the time. When children allege child abuse, fathers win 69% of the time, often despite extensive, corroborating evidence. Children's testimony is frequently written off as a product of the mother's coaching.[13]

Benoit's custody troubles began shortly after local police refused even to accept a report from her in 2011 and again in 2012. Eventually, when they allowed her to file a report, Benoit says police interrogated her for almost two full days, all while she says they questioned her rapist for just 30 minutes. At one point, Benoit told me that an officer looked her in the eye and said, "I believe you think you were raped." The subsequent police investigation that Benoit fought so hard for did little to change her situation. There was no conviction, which Benoit suspected was because she had been dating the man when he raped her. "They did not treat me like a victim. I still think about what they said to me all those years ago. These are the people that are supposed to help protect me."

In the span of seven years of some degree of co-parenting with her rapist between 2012 and 2019, the year that a judge's emergency order briefly stripped her rapist of custody (until the order was vacated in the summer of 2022), Benoit received protective orders against him each year. But despite this, his stalking and harassment never stopped, she told me. She was forced to move houses three times to protect herself and her child during this period, even though she was part of Arizona's Address Confidentiality Program, which bars her assailant from knowing where she lives. In court documents she shared with me, Benoit said she moved "strictly due to [my rapist] locating us by putting a tracker on our son" and that moving "is not an inexpensive thing."

Benoit's young child has suffered at the hands of her rapist, too. She shared photos with me revealing severe property damage he inflicted on the child's belongings, backing the child's allegations of physical and emotional abuse that he first made in 2019, resulting in the emergency protective order for the child. According to court documents filed by Benoit in 2021, when her rapist returned her son to her for the holiday on July 4, 2019, the child was missing "chunks [of hair] from the back of his head." Her son has endured such "severe trauma," she told me, that it's left him "years behind in school."

Around the spring of 2021, Benoit's rapist filed an appeal against the 2019 emergency order. At that point, the man all but confessed to the assault on-the-record to a court advisor, recounting that Benoit had "tried to push [him] off" during the nonconsensual encounter. But he resisted, he said, because he "was ready to orgasm." Yet, nothing became of the confession, and the retraumatizing, legal tug-of-war between Benoit and her son's biological father has continued to this day.

In 2023, the *New Yorker* spoke with a woman identified as Teresa, who was in a relationship when she was raped by her co-worker in 2016. Her relationship later ended, and she soon learned she was pregnant.[14] Teresa asked her rapist to take a paternity test to be certain and learned he was the twins' biological father. When Teresa's co-worker sought custody rights, a court battle ensued; the *New Yorker*'s Erin Overbey reviewed transcripts of the trial and said she "was shocked how quickly the judge seemed to assume that [Teresa] was just some disgruntled ex. It was almost as though once her twins were born, any consideration of those circumstances around their birth was relegated to this past."

"You have to understand, we're talking about a legal system, judges, prosecutors, social workers, many of whom just don't understand how a woman would act after becoming pregnant as a result of rape," Overbey said.

To this day, Teresa's rapist has some visitation rights over her children. "I've been told to get over the rape, and that happened in the past. I compared that to having a cancer diagnosis. You wouldn't tell somebody, 'Get over your cancer,'" she told Overbey.

Overbey also spoke to Lucy Guarnera, a psychology researcher at the University of Virginia who frequently interviews women who have endured custody battles with their rapists: "I had multiple participants talk about rapist fathers who, while they were pregnant, or shortly after they gave birth, threatened them or blackmailed them and said, 'Hey, if you go to police, or you continue cooperating with police, I am going to make your life a living hell. I am going to get custody and visitation access to your child, I'm never going to stop until I have full custody. You better drop that criminal case right now.' In some circumstances, this worked," Guarnera said. She continued, "I don't know if a 'power trip' is the word I'm looking for, but I think that's what it is and it's all just for power. Isn't that what sexual assault is? You just want to overpower your victim."

Custody Battles for Embryos and More

In 2023, then a few months after *Dobbs*, one particular tabloid headline caught my attention: "Anna Kendrick made embryos with 'toxic' ex who had feelings for someone else," it read. "I was with someone—this was somebody I lived with, for all intents and purposes my husband. We had embryos together, this was my person," Kendrick said on a podcast at the time. "And then about six years in, about somewhere around there, I remember telling my brother, when things had first kind of gone down, 'I'm living with a stranger.'"

Kendrick didn't disclose what had ever become of the embryos, but the timing of the revelation piqued my curiosity—and my concern—about the potential legal gray area surrounding frozen embryos after a couple separates, in a policy landscape that increasingly recognizes fetuses and embryos as children. The supposed personhood of embryos has become even more main-streamed since the previously mentioned Alabama Supreme Court ruling that recognized embryos as "extrauterine children"; in the aftermath of the case, within months, the U.S. Senate voted three times on a bill to codify a federal right to provide and receive IVF—each time, Senate Republicans blocked it. To be clear, if embryos are children, separated couples could find themselves in brutal custody battles over frozen embryos, or a pregnant spouse who crosses state lines without their abusive partner's permission could be charged with kidnapping.

The end of *Roe* has sparked growing concern among fer-tility clinics about how their work, which involves routine disposal of unused embryos during IVF, could be impacted by laws that legally recognize embryos as people. But even before *Dobbs*, courts and lawmakers have previously navigated convo-luted custody cases over separated couples' embryos, and the circumstances under which they can be destroyed. In 2018, Ari-zona's state Supreme Court determined that a woman couldn't use frozen embryos she'd made with her ex-husband. But in a chilling win for anti-abortion activists, the court ruled that the woman had to donate her unused embryos to couples or individuals struggling with fertility, so they wouldn't be left frozen or be destroyed. That same year, Arizona state lawmakers passed a bill requiring that in cases of disputed embryos, the embryos should be awarded to the party that's most likely to make them "develop to birth." Dana Sussman, senior vice president of Pregnancy Justice, called this law "concerning," as it could lead to someone getting custody of embryos even if their former partner doesn't consent to being a parent, or if their former partner is abusive and trying to wield the law to force a sustained relationship.

A few years earlier in 2015, a Superior Court judge in California sided with an ex-husband who wanted his shared embryos to be destroyed, even though his ex-wife wanted to use them. But in 2012 and 2016, in Pennsylvania and Illinois respectively, judges sided with women seeking possession of embryos over their exes' attempts to block them. The embryos had been created prior to both women undergoing cancer treatments threatening their fertility, and each judge determined the embryos were both women's only chance to have biological children. Over a decade earlier in 2000, a Massachusetts court ruled that "as a matter of public policy," a man who didn't want his ex-wife to develop their shared embryos should not be "[compelled] to become a parent against his or her will."

Then, in September 2022, a woman's ex-husband sued the abortion clinic that provided her with the procedure in 2018. He sued on behalf of the estate of her aborted embryo. Without evidence, the man claimed that doctors had failed to adequately inform his ex-wife of so-called safety risks associated with abortion, in accordance with state laws.

"I could see a universe in which an ex-partner, in an attempt to harass or terrorize or create fear in the pregnant person, would try to bring a wrongful death lawsuit against the pregnant person herself, in addition to the provider," Sussman said of the case at the time.

And while no legal dispute has yet emerged from the embryos Kendrick may still share with her ex, at least one famous ex-couple *has* gone to court over shared embryos. Sofia Vergara's ex, Nick Loeb, has sued the actress multiple times over frozen embryos the couple created together years earlier, seeking to force Vergara to be the biological parent of his kids against her will. In 2016, Loeb filed a lawsuit on behalf of plaintiffs "Emma" and "Isabella"—names he alone assigned to their unused embryos—and deliberately sued Vergara in the state of Louisiana, where embryos are recognized as "judicial persons." In the suit, Loeb claimed Vergara had "abandoned and chronically neglected" the embryos by freezing them for three years and denying them a chance to be born. Nothing ever came of Loeb's suit, but his legal harassment of Vergara inevitably stoked the frenzied support of anti-abortion and misogynist "father's rights" groups.

We can expect legal conflict surrounding embryos to continue: "Courts are often left to grapple with this and make judgment calls based on gleaning from other areas of law," Sussman told me. And now, they're doing so without the precedent of *Roe*. Post-*Dobbs*, fetal personhood presents an especially significant legal threat to survivors' safety, as it exposes them to exponentially greater risk of both state violence through policing and criminalization, and interpersonal violence, giving abusers a new avenue to wield the law to exert power over them.

In 2009, a California woman named Jessica Tebow and her husband were planning for the birth of their first child when a miscarriage and threat of a possibly fatal infection (which could also cause future infertility) forced her to have an emergency abortion. Tebow, who wrote about the experience in a *San Fran-*

cisco Chronicle op-ed in 2022, said she and her husband saved the miscarried embryo as they wanted to have a small, private ceremony to mourn and find closure.[15] But when her husband called the nearest funeral home and asked if they could pay for the cremation process for the embryo, they were told they needed to obtain a death certificate and also contact a coroner. Upon doing so, the couple piqued the suspicion of the Glendale Police Department, sparking an invasive, traumatic investigation—all as they continued to reel from the trauma of losing their wanted pregnancy. When Tebow was questioned by police about "the baby I had put in the freezer," she realized that police had broken into and searched her home. They had restrained her husband, threatened to arrest him, and confiscated their frozen, miscarried embryo, she wrote.

While the couple faced no criminal charges or arrest, and a coroner confirmed that what police had alleged was a dead baby was actually an embryo, the brush with law enforcement came with cascading consequences. Tebow lost her job. The shame and stigma surrounding their experience compelled the couple to move away and lose their community. Their story is a direct, gut-wrenching result of fetal personhood—the anti-abortion movement's endgame.

In 2023, Lauren Wranosky, a research associate at Pregnancy Justice, recounted to me the myriad fetal personhood cases she's reviewed in her work. An aspiring political candidate took legal action to try to change their birthday to the date of their conception to qualify for an age minimum requirement. In a child sexual abuse case, the perpetrator asked that their victim's age be calculated based on the date of conception to try to evade the highest maximum sentence, which can be imposed if a victim is under 14. Wranosky also raised that, again, in Mississippi and a handful of other states, you can be denied a divorce while pregnant out of consideration for the unborn "child." Further, recall that post-*Dobbs*, adults and children have been denied life-saving medications that can theoretically induce abortions or impact fertility, on the off-chance they're secretly pregnant. "What all of these achieve," Warnosky said, "is separating the fetus from the pregnant person," effectively prioritizing the life of a potential human over the actual human who's carrying it, regardless of that human's safety or their proximity to an abuser.

When an embryo is considered a "baby," this "[normalizes] the idea that a pregnant person is not their own person anymore, that they're subservient to the rights, individuality, and full personhood of a fetus," Sussman said. This can lead to especially horrific outcomes for pregnant people: "If their rights are secondary to the fetus, or at odds with the fetus, that lends to an environment in which violence—whether it's state violence like imprisonment, or interpersonal violence—can be committed against pregnant people with far less accountability."

When embryos are accorded legal standing as people, pregnant people's health and safety are endangered, particularly in a medical environment where they might need life-saving health care or treatment, sometimes after suffering from abuse. In 2004, when a Utah woman gave birth to twins and one was stillborn, she was arrested for fetal homicide for not going to the hospital soon enough.[16] In 2009, doctors determined a Florida woman was at risk of a miscarriage, and proceeded to keep her at the hospital against her will and force her to undergo an unwanted cesarean procedure. That same year, in Iowa, a pregnant mother of two was charged with attempted feticide after she fell down some stairs, miscarried, and doctors reported her to police because they misidentified her pregnancy as being in the third trimester. An Iowa statute defines termination of pregnancy in the third trimester as illegal.

In 2022, a Texas woman named Lizelle Herrera was arrested, jailed, and charged with homicide for allegedly self-managing an abortion with medication; Herrera was compelled by the hospital to have a c-section to remove the fetal remains. She was then reported to police by a health care professional she'd turned to for help. A decade earlier, in 2013, Purvi Patel was charged with feticide for allegedly self-managing an abortion—she, too, had been reported to police by her doctor. Per research from If/When/How in 2022, in most cases in which pregnant people faced criminal charges for self-managed abortion in the last 20 years, they were reported to law enforcement by health care workers and acquaintances. Laura Huss, a senior researcher at If/When/How and co-author of the report, cautioned to me that when patients know health care providers are policing them—namely, because their pregnancies are legally regarded as separate, sovereign beings—"that can only make people more afraid to get the care they need," and make pregnancy more dangerous.

Shortly after *Dobbs*, a pregnant woman in Texas sued for the right to drive in the carpool lane while pregnant to contest a traffic ticket she'd received. At the time, the case was hailed as a feminist statement poking a hole in anti-abortion hypocrisy. But legal experts cautioned about the dangerous doors that a lawsuit like this could open.

In 2021, Texas lawmakers introduced a bill to allow pregnant people to drive in carpool lanes—but the policy wasn't a victory for pregnant people at all, so much as it was a move toward legitimizing abortion bans by validating that life "begins at conception." Virginia Republicans introduced a similar bill in January 2023. Notably, in 2009, a New York woman was charged with manslaughter for not wearing a seatbelt and miscarrying during a car accident.

In 2022, House Republicans introduced a Child Tax Credit to give financial assistance to pregnant people. Later that same year, Senate Republicans introduced a bill to require fathers of embryos as young as one month to pay child support. A string of state legislatures including Oklahoma, Kansas, Kentucky, Georgia, Wisconsin, and other states introduced similar such bills in 2023 and 2024. Wranosky told me she's even seen the argument in court that imprisoning a pregnant person violates not their rights, but the "due process" rights of their embryo or fetus.

None of this has been floated in the interests of empowering or protecting pregnant people. This isn't the objective of fetal personhood. All of these bills and legal arguments are about legitimizing embryos as people; it's all a play to further strip pregnant people of their most basic rights, to treat them merely as vessels for babies, to be controlled by the state or abusive partners, to be threatened with criminalization—or, as we've seen, endless legal harassment from their abusers. This is the legal landscape that abortion bans have helped to create.

Chapter 4

Reproductive Coercion

In the first year after the *Dobbs* ruling, recall that the first public case of someone sentenced to jail time over their abortion involved a teenager in Nebraska who testified that she had a medication abortion to exit an abusive relationship. "I don't get the impression, from reading all the reports in the pre-sentence investigation report, that there was some kind of physical health issue that was going on," the judge, District Judge James Kube, told the young woman in court.[1] "I tried to talk to you about that a little bit, and you confirmed that you just didn't want this baby, you didn't want this pregnancy based on the person that got you pregnant." In other words, the judge didn't regard the young woman's abusive relationship as a valid reason (as if one needs such a thing) to have an abortion.

In 2024, Molly Voyles of Texas Council on Family Violence told me her organization found "more than 40% of Texas survivors say they have experienced at least one type of reproductive coercion," and that "reproductive coercion in Texas happens at three times the national average rate." This means "survivors experience unintended pregnancies, as well as other serious reproductive health issues, as a result of their partner's controlling behavior."

"There is undoubtedly a dangerous nexus between pregnancy and domestic violence," Voyles said.

In a HuffPost report published in March 2024, the director of a Texas-based abortion fund said that large swaths of their callers were experiencing domestic violence: "The amount of times I've heard from clients who say, 'He can't know I had an abortion,' or 'I can't have this child because I'll be tied to this person forever,' or 'The last time I was pregnant, that's when it was the worst.' It was all the time," Anna Rupani, executive director at Fund Texas Choice, said.[2] It was routine for the fund to ask callers if it was safe to call them back because so many of them were facing violence. Cathy Torres of Texas' Frontera Fund, an abortion fund serving undocumented people and residents along the Texas-Mexico border, detailed the plight of undocumented abortion seekers experiencing domestic violence: "If someone is undocumented, abusers will say, 'OK, I'll call ICE on you or I'll call customs.' That has always been the case. But now [post-Dobbs] they're just emboldened."

According to Julia Desangles, co-director of the abortion fund Florida Access Network (FAN), many of FAN's callers are domestic violence victims, which is why FAN trains its volunteers and employees to offer clients trauma-informed services. Abortion bans are often highly retraumatizing to sexual assault survivors, whose bodily autonomy and consent are yet again violated—this time by the state. Lauren Wilson, an organizer at Oklahoma's Roe Fund, told me in 2022 that this retraumatization can be exacerbated by the strenuous, sometimes dangerous journey of traveling out of state for care. She's heard from a volunteer who helped one Texas woman coming off an eleven-hour bus ride to Oklahoma (while abortion was still legal in Oklahoma, but banned by Texas' S.B. 8), during which the woman was forced to sit between two "older gentlemen"— one of whom was "very inappropriate towards her almost the entire time." Still, the Texas woman had no other option but to make the trek due to Texas' ban, all while carrying an unwanted pregnancy. "I don't think a lot of people realize the reality of that—that just to access basic health care, someone would have to go through the unimaginable," said Wilson, "[and] be in such vulnerable, traumatizing situations."

It's estimated that a tenth of people who have abortions do so to exit abusive, dangerous relationships. Between 6% and 22% of abortion patients report recently experiencing violence from an intimate partner prior to their abortion, per a 2014 survey.[3] A decade later, again, the National Domestic Violence Hotline reported that calls about reproductive coercion doubled between the fall of *Roe* in 2022 and the summer of 2023. Many calls involved abusive partners explicitly weaponizing abortion bans to control their victims. This is because state and inter-personal violence are inseparable from each other: Abortion bans are a form of state reproductive coercion, and on an inter-personal level, abusive partners also perpetrate reproductive coercion through a variety of means—for example, by tampering with their victims' birth control, blocking their access to abortion, pressuring them to have abortions, or otherwise exerting control over their reproductive decision-making.

In 2023, the Hotline said that the year before *Dobbs*, they received 1,230 calls about reproductive coercion; in the year after, the hotline received 2,442. Crystal Justice, chief external affairs officer for the Hotline, told me at the time that she'd grown accustomed to the harrowing cases of domestic violence from hotline callers over the years. But since *Dobbs*, Justice said that a few particular calls have stood out to her. One woman said her partner was intercepting her birth control pills after learning she was having them mailed to her. The woman eventually became pregnant but lived in a state where abortion is banned, and called the hotline desperate to learn her options.

The organization also heard from a caller whose partner didn't allow her to use contraception, then threatened to kill her after she became pregnant. Another caller became pregnant in a state that banned abortion shortly after her partner sexually assaulted her. Before *Dobbs*, Justice told me, one caller had a health condition that made pregnancy life-threatening for her; still, her abusive partner stole and sabotaged her birth control. He also stopped her from leaving their home. If such a situation arose today, and this individual managed to escape her home and see a doctor, would she even be able to receive an abortion?

"We've seen abusive partners weaponize the possible criminality of accessing abortion, or wrongfully tell a victim that if they do access abortion, they themselves could go to jail, or they'll report them to the police," Justice said. Pregnancy outcomes and self-managed abortion are heavily policed and *can* lead to criminal charges—but importantly, no abortion bans currently in effect criminalize the abortion patient.

The following year, in 2024, the Hotline published findings of a new survey of close to 3,500 domestic violence victims. As I detailed earlier, this survey found 5% of respondents—that's about 200 people—said abusive partners threatened to report them to police or other legal authorities for considering having an abortion. Another 5% said partners threatened to sue or take them to court if they sought abortion care. Many victims no longer know their rights around abortion. If/When/How's Sara Ainsworth told me in 2025 that many of the callers seeking help from her organization's Repro Legal Helpline don't realize that abortion bans don't punish patients. "That's not even understood by many journalists or doctors—these laws are very confusing, and there's this deeply ingrained idea that if abortion is illegal, therefore someone who seeks it or has one is engaging in criminal activity." That's given abusers significant leeway over victims.

Ainsworth pointed to laws like Louisiana's, enacted in 2024, which criminalizes possession of medication abortion except for those who are imminently about to take it. It was the first of its kind in the nation, and many legal experts have struggled to predict how it will be enforced. "Laws change all the time, court rulings change things all the time, new bills are introduced all the time. Even when laws don't pass, they enable abusers to make threats that are really believable. It's so hard to follow everything," Ainsworth said. "This requires a steady stream of analyzing and anticipating, then trying to distill that complicated information into public education for victims." All the while, "people experiencing domestic violence are experiencing it in real time and need help and information as soon as possible."

"Abusers could now use new laws, or confusion about those laws, to harass and threaten their partners. And the stigma of abortion bans creates a culture where abusers feel even more entitled to control and punish their intimate partners for their reproductive decisions," the Hotline's 2024 report states, noting that attacks on reproductive rights "put survivor's lives and safety at risk," and cause further harm by "revictimizing survivors and emboldening abusive partners." The Hotline's report emphasizes that "people have the constitutional right to travel to get abortion care in a state that protects abortion access"— but "getting away from an abuser (and, in some states, also having to pass through immigration checkpoints) to travel outside the state can be impossible." That's another way abortion bans endanger domestic violence victims: The survey shows that distance prevented 7% of respondents from accessing reproductive health care services. Reproductive health clinics have been shuttering across the country as a direct result of abortion bans. As we've seen, a study published in 2024 showed laws designed to shut down abortion clinics are associated with increased risk of intimate partner violence-related homicide in the community.

Relatedly, a third (32%) of the Hotline's survey respondents said they lack access to a medical professional who focuses on reproductive health or pregnancy. "When access to that is reduced, the risk rises," the Hotline's Marium Durrani said, pointing to how some respondents called supportive OB-GYNs a "lifeline": "A lot of clinics have closed down, a lot of victims are trapped and don't have means to travel. It's that much more dangerous." Domestic violence rates are also higher in abortion-banned states like Texas, Oklahoma, Idaho, and Florida, Justice said. The risk is even greater in rural, secluded parts of these states, where access to a doctor or OB-GYN is limited. Self-managing an abortion at home may not be a safe option for victims, either: The Hotline's survey revealed 7% of respondents said their partners prevented them from using abortion pills. These respondents detailed how their partners blocked them by threatening to commit suicide, lighting the pills on fire, physically locking them up, or threatening to harm the respondents and their families if they went through with their abortions.

About a quarter (23%) of respondents to the survey said their current or former partner pressured them into becoming pregnant. Thirteen percent said their current or former partner used or threatened violence while they were pregnant. And 10% of respondents said abusive partners used or threatened violence if they expressed that they wanted an abortion. Durrani told me that "sadly," these experiences reflect "what we already know about how abusers weaponize pregnancy."

One respondent to the survey told the Hotline her partner "knowingly and forcefully kept having sex after [my] consent was withdrawn." She "became pregnant as a result of rape" and wanted to take emergency contraception but had no means of transportation to access it and "feared trying to go on my own, of what he would have tried to do if I left." The window passed for her to be able to take plan B, and she got pregnant. Another respondent said that her partner "got me pregnant deliberately against my will after I made it clear I didn't want kids. I believe he did it to keep me trapped and tied to him." Another respondent recounted that three months into dating her partner, he stopped her from getting refills on her birth control, exerted control over her health appointments, and never wore condoms or would remove them without her consent. At one point, he beat and raped her: "He kept saying I was going to be the mother of his child," she wrote. She was able to escape the relationship soon after this, "but he would threaten me over text, saying if I killed our baby, he would hurt me." The respondent didn't become pregnant, but it's clear that if she had, her vulnerability to violence would have increased exponentially.

"I was forced to have sex, unwanted and unprotected. I was often told he'd 'pull out,' but then he wouldn't. He wanted me pregnant. When I became pregnant (which he wanted and I did not), I went on my own to Planned Parenthood to terminate the pregnancy," another respondent wrote. But "it took so long" for her abuser "to allow me to leave the home alone, let alone to PP," that she was much further along in her pregnancy than she wished to be at that point.

Ainsworth said she's heard from callers to the Repro Legal Helpline who can't leave their abuser because they share kids, or "were in an abusive relationship for a very short time, tried to get away, but then got pregnant because of birth control sabotage, and now, under an abortion ban, they're terrified." Ainsworth always knew the disastrous impact abortion bans would have on domestic violence victims and advocates who try to help them. "But it's one thing to know, and another to have to say to someone, 'You live in a state where you're more likely to be crim-inalized than the person who's abusing you.' It's devastating."

Forcing pregnancy on victims is a desirable goal for abusers, Durrani explained to me, because it offers an opportunity to entrap victims in a long-term way—and abortion bans have made this objective more attainable than ever. The Turnaway Study, mentioned in Chapter 2, for instance, found that people who are denied wanted abortion care are at significantly greater risk of long-term domestic violence.

In the Hotline's 2024 report, the organization also cites one of its previous surveys, which found 70% of respondents who called the police on their abusers regretted their decision and wouldn't contact the police again. Between this long-existing fear of police, and the role of recent abortion bans in empowering abusers to threaten to call law enforcement over their victims' reproductive decisions, Durrani contended that all of this is con-nected: "It shows the legal system, abortion bans, can be used as a tool of abuse. We're seeing the rise of litigation abuse," she said, citing the recent cases brought forth by lawyer Jonathan Mitchell. "It's terrifying on a whole new level, just the threat of being sued, further entangled with your abuser, in an adversarial system that forces victims to relive all kinds of trauma."

This data tells us that while abortion bans are "in and of them-selves state-based reproductive coercion," as Justice put it, they also create the optimal conditions for reproductive coercion to be perpetrated by abusive partners, too.

Political Disempowerment in the Home and Beyond

Almost half (42%) of respondents to the Hotline's 2024 survey said they didn't seek help for the reproductive coercion they experienced. One of the respondents said they didn't associate acts of reproductive coercion with abuse until encountering the survey, which Durrani told me is common: "When people think of gender-based violence, they tend to think of rape or physical abuse—there are lots of different ways people don't realize abuse can take place, whether it's reproductive coercion or financial abuse," she explained. "There's lots of different systems survivors interact with that abusers can exploit." In 2021, the California legislature passed a law that added reproductive coercion to the state's civil definition of domestic violence. This level of recognition and broadening of our understanding of gender-based violence, Durrani said, can be "life-saving."

Incidentally, in 2021, I spoke to Jane Stoever, a law professor and director of the University of California, Irvine Domestic Violence Clinic and the university's Initiative to End Family Violence. Stoever helped write the California law. She told me that she often counsels survivors of domestic violence who don't even realize they experienced sexual assault because it was perpetrated by a long-term partner. They certainly aren't aware that domestic violence includes their partner sabotaging their access to birth control or other forms of reproductive coercion.

About 15% of women experiencing physical violence from a male partner also report experiencing birth control sabotage. Per the American College of Obstetricians and Gynecologists, a quarter of adolescent girls experiencing intimate partner violence reported that their abusive partners have attempted to nonconsensually impregnate them by interfering with their contraception. Among adolescent mothers on public assistance who experienced intimate partner violence, 66% reported birth control sabotage by an abusive partner.[4]

These acts are typically underreported because many victims may not realize their partner's actions constitute domestic violence: "Reproductive coercion is typically not the only type of abuse experienced in a relationship in which intimate partner violence is present, and it can be challenging to reveal," Stoever said. "Naming a problem is often the first step in addressing it. Naming the behavior enables and empowers survivors to identify what they have experienced as abuse."

Through reproductive coercion, interpersonal abuse intersects with state violence: As I referenced earlier, my book *Survivor Injustice* explored how nearly every state that had recently imposed some form of abortion ban, even prior to *Dobbs*, also had a reported domestic violence rate higher than the national average.

The impact is simultaneous disempowerment, not just in the home and in one's body, but in one's ability to participate in public life and exercise a political voice. To be entrapped in an abusive relationship or abusive domestic situation is to suffer from political violence; many abuse victims are unable to vote, organize, control their finances, or exercise any amount of agency within their own lives, let alone in their communities. Again, the National Sexual Violence Resource Center notes that the lifetime economic cost of rape across all U.S. victims stands at nearly $3.1 trillion. Years after experiencing sexual violence, survivors have health care costs that are 19% higher than costs for women who haven't been abused, per the organization's research.

Laws and policy outcomes that benefit abusers and harm abuse victims are created and maintained through the political disempowerment of victims. Central to both interpersonal gender-based violence and state gender-based violence is the dehumanization of the victim, the denial of their agency and citizenship: One Oklahoma lawmaker inadvertently said the quiet part aloud in 2017, five years before *Dobbs*, as he defended a bill to require consent of the father of the fetus for someone to have an abortion: "I understand that they feel like that is their body," he said of pregnant people. "I feel like it's separate—what I call them is, you're a 'host.'"

Violence at Anti-Abortion Centers

In 2013, Maleeha Aziz was 20 years old when she immigrated to the U.S. and faced an unplanned pregnancy. When she sought help from a loved one to find an abortion clinic, they inadvertently directed her to an anti-abortion crisis pregnancy center—an organization that exists almost solely to target, prey on, and lie to potential abortion seekers to stop them from having abortions, all while posing as an abortion clinic. Most of the people who visit CPCs are young and low-income, lured by the misleading offer of free ultrasounds and other resources. CPCs then subject them to torrents of disinformation with the end goal of convincing someone against abortion or delaying them to the extent that it may be impossible to get one.[5]

Speaking to me in 2024, Aziz recalled a particularly chilling moment when a crisis pregnancy center worker told her she needed an ultrasound. Like most CPC workers, this person wasn't a medically licensed health care worker, but Aziz didn't know this at the time. When Aziz explained she was uncomfortable due to past trauma as a sexual assault survivor, she says the CPC worker told her that, as a pregnant woman, she "[needed] to learn to deal with pain." Aziz did eventually get her abortion—the first of two, before choosing to have her daughter in 2019—but only after the anti-abortion "clinic" first lied that it was too late for her to get one in Texas (it wasn't), forcing her to "spend money I didn't have" and travel to Colorado for the procedure, all while suffering from severe morning sickness.

Aziz said she sees her identities, as a survivor of gender-based violence, an immigrant, and, at the time, a financially insecure young woman, as key factors in why and how the fake clinic targeted her. "They definitely prey on vulnerable people specifically," Aziz explained. "Had I known that was a fake clinic all those years ago, would I let them touch me? Absolutely not. I wouldn't have even gone in there. I was deceived and violated." Aziz said she felt she had to allow the CPC workers to perform the invasive ultrasound on her because she thought they were medical professionals. "But they weren't, so it's not OK that they did that. That's violent in and of itself—that they touched me under false pretenses, did all of these things to further traumatize me—that's absolutely violence."

At one point while Aziz was at the crisis pregnancy center, she recounted that she felt physically trapped at the facility. Employees at the center had her sit in a room "through 30 minutes of torture watching this [anti-abortion] propaganda video," keeping the door closed and making her feel she "could not leave." Further, the anti-abortion clinic workers made use of every minute she spent at the facility to collect personal information about her. Believing she was at a health care facility, Aziz provided everything they asked for. "To this day, I don't know what they used it for, if they still have it," she said. For months, even after she had her abortion, the center continued to "call and harass" her until she blocked their number. "The whole time I was there, they kept talking to me, trying to make me feel like they're my friends so I would tell more about myself—actual health care workers have never asked me the things they asked, like about my family, my life."

Aziz went on to serve as the deputy director of the Texas Equal Access (TEA) abortion fund. After her experience at the CPC, she saw her advocacy for reproductive justice and identity as a survivor as "interconnected." She didn't become pregnant and seek abortion due to sexual assault, but she sought to end her pregnancy to leave an emotionally abusive relationship. "As a survivor, as someone who's had abortions, those identities live on with you," she said. Both experiences motivated and shaped her urgent activism for bodily autonomy—and her understanding of CPCs and anti-abortion state governments as conjoined perpetrators of gender-based violence. Several states have introduced or passed bills like Kentucky's required transvaginal ultrasound law in 2019, which mandates that abortion seekers receive ultrasounds before they can have the procedure, even though there's no medical necessity for this. It's an under-discussed form of state violence and manipulation.

Since *Dobbs*, the "[crisis pregnancy centers'] agenda hasn't changed," Aziz said. "They will continue to prey on vulnerable people and provide them with misinformation." CPCs receive more state funding than ever, she continued, money that could support the very pregnant people whom CPCs prey on. In the first two years after *Dobbs* alone, state governments poured close to $500 million into CPCs. The same states that have totally banned or severely restricted abortion, like Texas and Florida, have poured the most money into CPCs post *Dobbs*.[6]

Even more concerning, there's still no clarity about how anti-abortion centers use abortion seekers' data and personal information: Most individual CPCs are cogs in an enormous anti-abortion machine, with deep connections to the most powerful, well-funded anti-abortion organizations in the world. They often use the same back-end digital management system provided by one such organization, Heartbeat International, to store and potentially share people's data, which is especially ominous in a post-*Dobbs* climate where pregnancy and abortion are shrouded in criminal suspicion. Heartbeat International's

Option Line chat program, used by most CPCs to communicate with potential abortion seekers, states in its terms of use that "all remarks" sent through Option Line can be used "for any and all purposes . . . appropriate to the mission and vision of Option Line." One state lawmaker speaking in a 2024 documentary about CPCs called *Preconceived* characterized CPCs as "the surveillance center of the anti-abortion movement." The surveillance of pregnancy and abortion, as I'll detail in the following chapter, will render unsaid numbers of pregnant people and domestic violence survivors vulnerable to the threat of criminalization—a threat that's always existed and has been exacerbated post-*Dobbs*.

Aziz's experience at a crisis pregnancy center presents a harrowing glimpse at the inextricability of state and interpersonal abuse, at how pregnant victims of abuse can be deliberately preyed on by state-funded institutions like anti-abortion centers, then subjected to medical violence and state sexual assault. Her story is an encapsulation of colluding forms of violence targeting pregnant survivors, and a snapshot of an experience and vulnerability that *Dobbs* has only deepened.

Chapter 5

The Criminalization of Survival and Pregnancy

In the summer of 2024, the National Domestic Violence Hotline's reporting revealed a new power that abusers had gained through abortion bans and confusion about the specifics of these laws: Close to 200 respondents said abusive partners threatened to report them to police or other legal authorities for considering having an abortion. Another 200 said abusive partners threatened to sue or take them to court if they sought abortion care. If/When/How's Sara Ainsworth told me that "most of the people experiencing criminal and legal threats over their pregnancy, who call [If/When/How's Repro Legal Helpline], are also experiencing domestic abuse." This, of course, can contribute to the pipeline of abuse survivors who find themselves incarcerated.

At the end of 2023, Brittany Watts, a Black woman in Ohio, faced felony charges for "abuse of a corpse" after miscarrying 22 weeks into her pregnancy in September that year, allegedly while using the restroom and then flushing the fetal remains down her toilet. The remains were ultimately uncovered by local law enforcement—but only after a nurse who suspected Watts of having an abortion reported her to authorities.

Watts faced the felony charge despite a forensic pathologist testifying that her fetus was not born alive and died before passing through the birthing canal; further, the expert said the fetus was "nonviable because [Watts] had premature ruptured membranes—her water had broken early—and the fetus was too young to be delivered." Watts' defense attorney, Tracy Timko, told reporters that her client "learned days before" her miscarriage that this outcome "was inevitable and that the fetus could not survive outside the womb due to gestational age." Still, she was unable to receive abortion care.

But the county assistant prosecutor argued that "the issue isn't how the child died, when the child died, it's the fact that the baby was put into a toilet, large enough to clog up a toilet, left in that toilet and she went on [with] her day." (To be clear: Fetal remains from a miscarriage are not a "child" or "baby," and this language is both inaccurate and dangerous.) Still, Warren Municipal Court Judge Terry Ivanchak determined to move the case forward, dismissively shrugging off the matter of "the exact legal status of this fetus/corpse/body/birthing tissue/whatever it is." At the time, Timko told me, "Brittany suffered a tragic and dangerous miscarriage that jeopardized her own life. Rather than focusing on healing physically and emotionally, she was arrested and charged with a felony." State law, Timko argued, "does not support criminalizing someone for a pregnancy loss."

Timko was right: If/When/How's Farah Diaz-Tello told me that a case like Watts' is "shocking but not unexpected," as her organization's research shows "prosecutors are looking for ways to punish people when the law doesn't really allow it" as applied to pregnancy. Watts' case was also inseparable from her identity as a Black woman: "We have a young Black woman who's being punished for something that happens to people across the country all the time," Diaz-Tello said. "It's no coincidence, the scrutiny and judgment that's been placed on her for something that in other circumstances would be considered a tragedy. Yet when we're talking about a Black woman, we're treating it like it's a crime."

Pregnancy Justice's Dana Sussman pointed out that the felony charge against Watts represented a textbook "misapplication" of the law, as "abuse of a corpse" charges don't apply to miscarriage or pregnancy. As many as a quarter of pregnancies end in miscarriage and there's no legal handbook for what to do upon this common pregnancy outcome. Watts' case, she argued, shows that "you don't need an abortion ban to criminalize pregnancy." Sussman stressed that about 97% of criminal charges for pregnancy outcomes that she's seen have been for "murder, manslaughter, feticide, child endangerment, abuse of a corpse" rather than abortion laws.

Still, cultural hostility to abortion is inextricably linked with state policing of pregnancy. Many of the cases Sussman and Pregnancy Justice have tracked involve "suspicion or a question about whether someone intentionally sought to end their pregnancy," with criminal charges doled out to "punish someone for possibly engaging in this behavior." Recall that in 2023, a Nebraska teen was sentenced to 90 days in jail for a self-managed abortion to escape an abusive relationship the prior year. The teen pleaded guilty not for having had an abortion, but for a felony charge of concealing or abandoning a dead body.

It's common for people who miscarry to flush fetal remains like Watts did. When people who experience miscarriage or stillbirth dispose of fetal remains through other means, such as burying the remains or bringing them to the hospital, Pregnancy Justice has found these individuals may *still* face criminal charges. In 2017, years before *Dobbs*, a teenager in Ohio was charged with aggravated murder, involuntary manslaughter, child endangerment, and gross abuse of a corpse after burying a stillborn fetus in her backyard. A year later, a Wisconsin woman faced similar charges for disposing of stillborn twins. And the year after *that*, a Virginia woman was convicted and briefly jailed for "concealing a dead body" after disposing of remains from a stillbirth.

Criminal charges stemming from pregnancy loss long predate *Dobbs*. Per a report from Pregnancy Justice in September 2023, there were about 2,000 such cases between 1973 (when *Roe* was decided) and the summer of 2022, when the court decided *Dobbs*.[1] Around the same time this report was published, Pregnancy Justice president Lourdes Rivera told me the organization is "busier than ever post-*Dobbs*," and at that point, had already tracked dozens of cases of pregnancy-related criminalization in 14 states in 2023 alone. Like Watts' experience, very few of these cases directly involved abortion laws. But, as Sussman put it, abortion bans ultimately contribute to "creating a specter of suspicion and criminal framework around pregnancy," as well as "a culture of fear and confusion that's very intentional."

We've already seen this at work. As I detailed earlier, from June 2022 to June 2023—the first year after *Dobbs*—the highest ever number of pregnancy-related prosecutions were documented in a single year. Pregnancy Justice's 2024 report showed 198 cases involved charges of some form of child abuse, neglect, or endangerment, while other cases involved charges of homicide, abuse of a corpse, alleged substance use, and more. In some of these cases, the pregnant person's research or apparent contemplation of abortion are recorded in their case files—possibly to be weaponized as evidence of "intent to kill" their fetus before miscarrying their pregnancies.

Diaz-Tello explained to me that Watts' case "[had] everything and nothing to do with [*Dobbs*]." In January 2024, an Ohio jury ultimately dropped the charge against Watts in the wake of substantial public pressure (and the fact that there was no real case against her). Of course, in many ways, the damage was done: Her face, name, and story had been broadcasted far and wide, and she'd been retraumatized by the medical and criminal systems.

Pregnancy Justice's 2024 report also showed that most criminal charges alleged substance use during pregnancy (for legal and illegal substances alike), in what Rivera called "an extension of the racist War on Drugs," which disproportionately polices Black and brown mothers and pregnant people. In 2024, the criminal justice organization the Marshall Project found that hospitals across the country are using inaccurate pee-in-a-cup drug tests resulting in pregnant people and new mothers losing custody or facing criminal investigation over false positives—including for merely eating poppyseeds. Later that same year, the Marshall Project reported on numerous cases of hospital workers reporting pregnant and postpartum people to police for testing positive for drugs that the hospital itself gave them, leading to women being investigated by the state or losing custody of their children over misunderstandings. At least 27 states require hospitals to alert child welfare agencies about pregnant people's positive drug tests or potential drug exposure in babies—but none require the hospitals to confirm the veracity of tests before reporting patients.

About 40% of people who were investigated by police for self-managing abortions between 2000 and 2020 were reported by healthcare workers, per an If/When/How report from 2022 that tracked 61 different cases.[2] Each of these cases, but especially those flagged to police by health care workers, is a failure of public health, dissuading people who may need medical help from seeking care within a health system that prioritizes surveillance and punishment over service.

Rivera linked criminal charges against pregnant people to rising maternal mortality, because patients who struggle with substance use disorders are afraid to go to the doctor. Pregnancy Justice found 121 of the 210 criminal cases documented from June 2022 to June 2023 stemmed from health care workers reporting their patients. The organization's report warned that since *Dobbs*, anti-abortion lawmakers are only creating new avenues to criminalize pregnancy outcomes. In 2023 alone, 17 states introduced 22 bills to try to police self-managed abortion. In 2024, Louisiana enacted a law to classify the most common, highly safe abortion pills as a "controlled dangerous substance," even as one of the pills, misoprostol, is crucial to stop postpartum hemorrhaging and prevent maternal mortality. Louisiana's law offers an exception for pregnant people who are about to use the pills to end a pregnancy—but as one legal expert told me in 2024, the process to determine this would be "incredibly invasive and intrusive," if not impossible. Lawmakers in Texas, Indiana, and other states introduced similar bills in 2025. All of this is meant to push medication abortion out-of-reach and expand the options available to the state to criminalize pregnancy. Pregnancy Justice's legal director Karen Thompson raised to me that laws like Louisiana's can be weaponized by abusive partners or ex-partners to call the police on their victim for simply owning abortion pills.

In 2023, Biden's Health and Human Services Department submitted a proposed rule change that would prevent patients' medical information from being used to investigate, sue, or prosecute patients and providers for seeking reproductive care. Of course, pregnancy-related criminalization also stems from a public education crisis: Too many health care workers seem to think it's their job to report pregnant people to the cops when it isn't at all.

Following the Biden administration's proposed rule change, 19 anti-abortion state attorneys general pushed back with a frightening opposition letter, insisting cops have a right to investigate pregnant people's potential abortions and access their medical information even across state lines. The letter argued the Biden administration proposal "would unlawfully interfere with States' authority to enforce their laws"—in this case, abortion bans. The top law enforcement officials in these 19 states said they were concerned with their own residents traveling out of state for abortions, even though this is legal: "The proposed rule would thus curtail the ability of state officials to obtain evidence of potential violations of state laws . . . The statute does not empower HHS to shield from authorities evidence of legal wrongdoing under state law based simply on a claimed connection to 'health care.'" Vice President JD Vance signed a similar letter when he served in the U.S. Senate in 2023.

Watts' is one story: It's part-and-parcel of an extensive history and ongoing crisis. In 2019, a Black woman named Marshae Jones was briefly jailed in Alabama for losing a pregnancy after being shot in the stomach, blamed by prosecutors for engaging in reckless behavior and getting into a fight. And there's also the case of Kelsey Carpenter, a California mother who was incarcerated after tragic complications with a home birth in 2020 led to her being charged with murder and felony child abuse, imprisoned from 2021 until 2023.

Carpenter, a survivor of child sexual abuse, had previously lost custody of her two children due to struggles with substance abuse, which, according to family members, began when Carpenter struggled to process the violence she'd survived.[3] Carpenter feared her baby would be taken from her by the state if she had a hospital birth, since she'd lost custody of her first two children after testing positive for drugs. So, she prepared extensively for the home birth, consulting a midwife, and even naming her then-unborn child Kiera. But after giving birth, Carpenter lost consciousness due to significant blood loss, and when she awoke, found her newborn unresponsive. She called 911 after unsuccessfully performing CPR on the infant. Carpenter was then taken to the police station and, while still in shock and significant physical pain, she was arrested and charged with killing her child, facing the threat of life in prison. A county coroner deemed the newborn's death an accident in the autopsy from 2020, and a California law that took effect in 2023 prohibits criminal charges for pregnancy outcomes. Despite this, the county district attorney's office pushed its case against Carpenter for years. In 2023, Carpenter's attorney Amber Fayerberg described the then-ongoing case to me as both a "harbinger and a symptom" of life without *Roe*. Carpenter's case drew national media attention after *Dobbs* brought renewed public scrutiny to the mistreatment, policing, and criminalization of pregnant people in the U.S., and by the end of 2023, prosecutors dismissed the murder charge against Carpenter, approving her release from jail the following month.[4]

Still, Carpenter can't meaningfully be compensated for the years she spent in jail—years apart from her children, years compounding the trauma of losing her child with state punishment. Hers is another story of a survivor violated and terrorized by the criminal legal system for the outcome of her pregnancy.

White Supremacy and the Criminalization of Pregnancy

White supremacy is an indelible piece of pregnancy-related criminalization. In 2021, almost a year before *Dobbs*, a 21-year-old Oklahoma woman was convicted of first-degree manslaughter after losing a pregnancy in her second trimester. Brittney Poolaw, a Native American member of the Comanche Nation, experienced a miscarriage and stillbirth in January 2020 and was sentenced in October to four years in prison. Poolaw's sentencing came after a medical examiner confirmed that her 15 to 17-week fetus had congenital abnormalities and tested positive for methamphetamine.

It's not a coincidence that Oklahoma has the second highest population of Indigenous people in the country, paired with especially stringent state policing of pregnancy and abortion. In 2017, one Oklahoma district attorney announced heightened measures to prosecute pregnant people who are alleged to have used criminalized drugs, namely by weaponizing the state's felony child neglect laws.[5] And just as data shows non-white people experience higher rates of stillbirths, miscarriage, and pregnancy complications than white people, state surveillance and criminalization of these outcomes—especially where drug use is alleged to be a factor—isn't race-neutral, either. Consequently, people of color and especially Native American people like Poolaw have historically faced higher rates of pregnancy and drug-related criminalization.

Twenty-three states and the District of Columbia maintain laws that equate drug exposure during pregnancy with child abuse, while 25 states and D.C. require health professionals to report suspected prenatal drug use, according to tracking by Guttmacher Institute.[6] In 38 states, "fetal assault" laws define an embryo or fetus as the potential victim of a crime. According to one report from 2012, about 2.5% of U.S. adults in addiction treatment are Native American,[7] though Native American people account for about 1% of the total population.[8] One study of 342 Native American patients at a hospital near the Great Lakes found 34.5% of their pregnancies were "substance-exposed."[9] This renders them disproportionately vulnerable to substance use-related pregnancy policing.

Insidious policies that criminalize substance use during pregnancy can also be traced to the distinctly racist, anti-Black War on Drugs. The myths and propaganda of the 1980s public health panic known as the "crack epidemic" saw Black pregnant people routinely subjected to mandated, nonconsensual drug-testing, with positive drug tests erroneously and cruelly treated as proof of child neglect and grounds to separate parents from their newborns, or criminalize rather than offer support to struggling pregnant people.[10] Pregnant Indigenous people remain exposed to greater risk of criminalization across the country, as they're more likely to use state-sponsored public health and social services programs, most of which impose mandated reporting policies for suspected drug use.

Tribes across the U.S. maintain their own legal approaches to address substance use during pregnancy, and a 2020 review of available tribal laws from the *AMA Journal of Ethics* found substance use during pregnancy is criminalized in most tribes, with varying responses and penalties. The *Journal* specifies that tribes like Navajo Nation and White Earth Nation mandate substance use treatment programs, while tribes like the Little River Band of Ottawa Indians and Standing Rock Sioux Tribe treat substance use during pregnancy as child abuse. Melissa Rose, an Akwesasne Mohawk midwife who works with Indigenous Women Rising's birthing fund to provide care to Indigenous pregnant people across New Mexico, told me in 2021 that the disproportionate threat of criminalization that Indigenous pregnant people face compounds with a range of other oppressions. Cases like Poolaw's don't occur in a vacuum: "In general, access to health care for our communities is already not great, so add on top of it, these fears for criminalization that create barriers," she said. "It does contribute to these unsafe outcomes" when Indigenous people avoid seeking prenatal care for fear of being reported to police and criminalized. Consequently, they face higher risk of pregnancy-related complications or even pregnancy loss, which can place them in the crosshairs of the criminal legal system, too.

Pregnancy and abortion-related criminalization—like all criminalization—is indelibly rooted in white supremacist violence. The outcomes are far-reaching, from the violence of incarceration to the violence of a punishing health system that, for some communities, is more likely to surveil and punish than offer health care.

Pregnancy and the Surveillance State

Shortly after Texas enacted S.B. 8—the abortion ban enforced by citizens spying on and policing each other—in 2021, Texas Right to Life launched a snitch hotline calling for "tips" about people they suspected to be seeking or helping people seek abortions. This hotline was immediately inundated with spam and memes. But aside from this almost comical show of incompetence, the threat of anti-abortion surveillance targeting anyone who seeks, provides, or helps someone obtain an abortion, or experiences any pregnancy-related complications, grows by the day.

Post-*Dobbs*, the anti-abortion movement has increasingly relied on enforcement through mechanisms like censorship and by compelling communities to turn on or refuse to help each other. Tennessee lawmakers, for example, have introduced legislation to try to allow family members of people who receive abortion pills in the mail to sue individuals who sent the pills, even if from a state where it's legal to do so, for $5 million. The bill's author called this "a reasonable amount" and said the bill is not extreme because Tennessee's wrongful death statute already includes "unborn children." In 2023, Texas and South Carolina introduced bills to ban internet providers from hosting websites that include information about seeking help from abortion funds and ordering abortion pills. In 2024, the U.S. Senate passed KOSA (the Kids Online Safety Act), which claims to protect children on the internet, but could instead be used by anti-abortion state attorneys-general to block online abortion information by threatening to prosecute internet providers that platform pro-abortion rights websites.

A range of other policies and threats from anti-abortion lawmakers are meant to scare communities into abandoning each other. After *Dobbs*, Alabama's attorney general threatened to charge anyone who helps someone travel out of state for abortion—which is legal—with a "criminal conspiracy." Alabama abortion funds and reproductive health providers soon sued. The leader of one fund told me the attorney general's threats, which stopped funds from being able to directly help callers, has been a disaster—in particular, for abuse victims. Jenice Fountain, executive director of the Alabama-based reproductive justice group Yellowhammer Fund, claimed that when pregnant people are forced to remain pregnant by the state's ban, sometimes they still need to travel out of state anyway: "We'll hear from domestic violence victims who have to escape or leave the state to give birth so their partner doesn't harm them, or their pregnancy, or their kid. That's just becoming a day-to-day reality." Robin Marty, director of a reproductive care clinic in the state, told *The Meteor* in 2024 that Alabama's anti-abortion policies are aimed at "completely and utterly isolating the person who is pregnant, because if you cut them off from information and any sort of assistance, then you have essentially isolated her and forced her to do what you want. And let's be honest, that's what domestic abusers do: isolate and then abuse and force them into what you want."[11]

Anti-abortion lawmakers want abortion seekers isolated and afraid, and for those who would otherwise help them to be intimidated by the threat of state surveillance and criminalization.

Digital surveillance has played a recurring role in allowing the state to collect evidence against pregnant people who come to the attention of law enforcement, with more success than Texas Right to Life's failed snitch hotline. Anti-abortion groups are already taking advantage of digital platforms to spy on people, for example, reportedly using mobile geo-fencing technology to bombard patients at or en route to clinics with targeted anti-abortion propaganda. Cynthia Conti-Cook, technology fellow at the Ford Foundation who focuses on gender, racial and ethnic justice, and author of "Surveilling the Digital Abortion Diary," told me in 2021 that this practice can be adopted by law enforcement agencies, using what are called "reverse geo-fence warrants." Cops "can ask Google for everyone within the radius of a specific location, at a specific time, based on their phones," then "create a lineup from that to investigate crimes in a specific location and generate possible leads from that." She continued, "Often with these surveillance and forensic technologies, there's large loopholes for law enforcement, for the legal system, to be able to operate within."[12]

There is extensive precedent for online search histories regarding medication abortion and abortion self-management options being wielded as evidence to land people like Lattice Fisher, a Black mother of three living in Mississippi, in jail. Fisher experienced a stillbirth that prosecutors tried to prove had instead been a live birth. Prosecutors successfully argued that Fisher had killed her own baby, citing her previous online searches for abortion pills as evidence of her "motive." She was incarcerated in 2018, but charges against her were eventually dropped two years later. Purvi Patel, an Indian-American woman in Indiana, was jailed and charged with infanticide in 2015 for allegedly inducing an abortion after her online purchase of abortion pills was used as evidence against her. The prosecution cited

Patel's private text messages with a friend, confiding that she was pregnant and searching for medication abortion online. Of course, using medication abortion was and is legal—the charge against Patel was contradictory: If she had an abortion, as the prosecution tried to demonstrate with her texts and search history, how did she also "kill" a born, living infant?

In May 2022, within hours of leaked news that the Supreme Court would end *Roe*, VICE reported that a location data firm had been selling the private information of people visiting abortion clinics. The firm soon after announced it would discontinue this practice. But the ease with which location data firms across the country and around the world can access pregnant people's movements and behaviors—and consequently, their most private medical decisions—and sell this information to the highest bidder remains an ever-looming threat post-*Dobbs*.

As prosecutors weaponize and misuse "feticide" and child endangerment laws to target people who experience miscarriage or self-manage their abortions, people's digital footprints are increasingly being wielded as criminal evidence against them. State surveillance of pregnancy and abortion long preceded *Dobbs*: In 2019, the director of Missouri's health department was exposed for tracking Planned Parenthood patients' menstrual cycles on a spreadsheet. Forty-six states and D.C. require some form of reporting abortions to the state, while states with fetal burial laws typically require people to obtain death certificates for aborted fetuses, entering their abortions into the public record. Heartbeat International, the leading network of crisis pregnancy centers, has historically flooded Facebook and Google with targeted ads (the organization received $150,000 of free ads from Google in 2019)[13] and uses a chat system called Option Line for "abortion-minded" users who must identify themselves and their locations. Per Heartbeat's own stated terms of use, "all remarks" sent through the website can be used by the organization "for any and all purposes . . . appropriate to the mission and vision of Option Line." Thousands of anti-abortion centers across the country use Option Line. "Big data is revolutionizing all sorts of industries. Why shouldn't it do the same for a critical ministry like ours?" Heartbeat International has said of its data collection practices.

"Crisis pregnancy centers are basically the ultimate movement building tool of the anti-abortion movement," Kim Clark, an attorney at the gender justice legal advocacy group Legal Voice, warned me in the weeks leading up to *Dobbs*. Some of these "clinics" even have contracts with state governments to help collect data from callers seeking abortion care, in a conjoined effort to stalk, possibly criminalize, and force people to give birth. And because, in most cases, they provide no actual health care, they often aren't subject to the patient privacy standards set by the privacy law HIPAA, which prohibits medical providers from sharing patients' private medical data in most circumstances. In a 2022 report, an abortion rights group called The Alliance expressed concern with the role of anti-abortion centers in collecting criminal evidence against pregnant people: "CPCs are positioned to play a central role in surveillance of pregnant people in such a vigilante system. They exist, after all, to reach people experiencing unintended pregnancies, and collect extensive digital data on their clients and their reproductive histories."

Crisis pregnancy centers across the country receive millions in state funding. The ratio of crisis pregnancy centers to abortion-providing clinics in the U.S. stood at three to one before *Dobbs*. Their websites are key to their surveillance and data collection, and they're able to draw potential abortion seekers to their websites through prominent placement on search engines like Google. Shireen Shakouri, executive vice president of the reproductive rights research organization Reproaction, told me in 2022 that she's heard from people who live in communities with few or no abortion clinics, who see only crisis pregnancy centers pop up when they Google search for abortion clinics.

One CPC victim testified to the Expose Fake Clinics campaign, which educates the public about CPCs' lies, that after she left a facility, one CPC worker "began calling her almost daily and telling her aggressively that she would die, or end up in hell, or get very sick if she were to go through with the abortion." Some people who have been lured into anti-abortion centers told the campaign they were forced to sign contracts pledging to not have an abortion before they were permitted to leave the facility. Shakouri told me she's heard from reproductive health care providers whose patients have told them that, while they were inside CPCs, staff members "locked them in exam rooms and told them 'you're not leaving until you say you're not going to have an abortion.'" This is an apt metaphor for the paradigm of violence the anti-abortion movement is trying to create—one of surveillance, entrapment, and coercion.

Chapter 6

Trapped: Pregnancy in the Carceral System

In Wills County, Illinois, in 2020, a woman named Aliyah was just four weeks pregnant when she began her sentence at the county jail. Throughout her pregnancy, she lost 67 pounds, and recounted being put on the wrong medications without her consent. She was repeatedly denied medical appointments and recommended blood work. At one point, Aliyah was attacked by guards and almost thrown to the floor because she accidentally took a shower during a lockdown. She was repeatedly hand-cuffed and shackled during her pregnancy, and when she told guards she was pregnant, she claims they "called me a liar and said I was just fat," per her account in a report from the ACLU of Illinois published in 2024.[1]

And in a different county jail in Illinois, in 2021, an incarcerated woman identified as Paige suffered from a high-risk pregnancy and had even been shot shortly before starting her sentence. Once behind bars, she tried to get an abortion out of concern for her safety. Paige was already a mother to four kids and she'd had three previous C-sections which rendered her pregnancy more dangerous. "When I found out I was pregnant, I asked the jail about getting an abortion through the electronic messaging system. Their only reply to my request for an abortion was to send me back a message with a frowny face like this ' :/ ,'" Paige recounts in the report.

Per the report, even though abortion is and remains legal in the ostensibly blue state, there are no consistent policies around abortion access in Illinois jails county by county. The organization couldn't uncover clear policies on health care and resources for pregnant and menstruating incarcerated people in general, beyond wildly cruel policies requiring people to pay for their own abortions despite having no income. It doesn't help that prisons tend to be located in rural areas, far from the nearest abortion provider, and those seeking care are tasked with the sometimes impossible burden of locating a nearby clinic without resources or support.

It's no coincidence that Black, brown, and Indigenous people are overrepresented in prison populations, given the indelible legacies of slavery, white supremacy, and Jim Crow-era segregation laws that created the modern-day prison system, as well as the ongoing over-policing of communities of color. And the carceral system has always presented a crisis of a reproductive injustice. Criminal charges for pregnancy loss including abortion have significantly increased in recent years—again, the most charges in a single year were doled out after *Dobbs*, from June 2022 to June 2023.

Confusion about prison abortion laws isn't just an Illinois issue. Vague policies, or total lack of policies, or untenable mandates for incarcerated people to pay for their own abortions (and sometimes pay fees for the officer taking them to get the abortion) are a universal crisis across the U.S., including in states that supposedly protect reproductive rights. Approximately 3% of women in jail in the United States were pregnant in 2017, according to researchers at Johns Hopkins School of Medicine. In 2024, the Marshall Project reviewed pregnancy policies in 27 jails in twelve different states, and also found no consistent policies (or sometimes any policies at all) governing pregnancy and abortion access.

On top of a lack of basic rights to health care, incarcerated pregnant people also report suffering from distinctly cruel, dangerous mistreatment: In the same ACLU of Illinois report, one incarcerated woman, Shawna, recalled being forced to wear handcuffs through an ultrasound and other basic health services for her pregnancy while jailed in LaSalle County and Rock County, Illinois, in 2019. When she learned her pregnancy was high-risk because her placenta was dangerously close to her cervix, doctors recommended that she see a specialist. But she recounts, "The jail told me that they didn't have to send me to a specialist, because I was only entitled to the minimum level of care, and they could send me wherever they wanted, whether I was pregnant or not."

All of this is gender-based violence, from being unable to access abortion or prenatal care behind bars, to the horrific abuses pregnant people say they've experienced while they were incarcerated in state prisons. Prisons present another horrific dimension of state reproductive violence, inflicted on the most marginalized populations. This is only worsened by abortion bans, which render abortion access all but impossible in most prisons, and simultaneously create greater risk for pregnant people to wind up criminalized and incarcerated.

The state's policing of pregnancy contributes to the sexual assault-to-prison pipeline, through which 90% of incarcerated women survived gender-based violence before being imprisoned. And as If/When/How's Sara Ainsworth raised, most of the callers to her organization's hotline who are concerned about pregnancy-related criminal and legal threats are simultaneously victims of domestic abuse. Victims of sexual assault are substantially more likely than perpetrators to ever be incarcerated, and once in prison, they're at high risk of being sexually victimized again, often by the guards who are entrusted with state power over them. One study showed 60% of prison rapes are perpetrated by guards.[2] Taken together, feminist anti-carceral activists call this "state sexual assault," through which the state itself facilitates sexual violence on a person's being. Becki Truscott Kondkar, director of Tulane Law School Domestic Violence Clinic, regularly works with criminalized survivors—women who face criminal charges for circumstances related to abuse they experienced; she told me in 2024 that her work has shown her how "prisons replicate intimate partner violence on a larger scale," and "sometimes replicate the abusive circumstances that may have played a major role in someone's trajectory to prison. Sexual violence is ubiquitous in there."

Reproductive oppression and coercion are a feature of the carceral system: As recently as 2017, a judge in Tennessee offered to reduce jail time for incarcerated people, who are more likely to be poor people of color, if they opted to be sterilized. The offer ignored, or rather, exploited, that no person held captive by the state can meaningfully consent. Azhar Gulaid, a policy analyst at Urban Institute, told me in 2022 that it's possible coerced sterilizations happen more often than we realize in prisons, building on the white supremacist history of forced sterilizations carried out by the state. "Despite laws and protections, in actuality, on the ground, prison staff have so much discretion that then leads to this."

In 2024, *Gothamist* reported that the state of New York faced 719 civil lawsuits between 1976 and 2023 alleging sexual violence on Rikers Island. Pregnant incarcerated people were particularly vulnerable to violence.[3] At least nine women alleged that they were sexually assaulted or raped while pregnant. One of these women reported that her doctor gave her a gynecological exam that was so violent her cervix ruptured.

In New York state, the Adult Survivors Act, originally passed in May 2022, temporarily expanded the statute of limitations for sex crimes, granting victims a one-time opportunity to file civil suits. The bill also crucially allowed victims to file suits about mistreatment in state facilities including prisons. One law firm, Slater Slater and Schulman, which specializes in representing abuse victims, told the *New York Times* in November 2022 that the firm, alone, expected to file 750 individual civil lawsuits on behalf of incarcerated women who allege they were sexually assaulted by prison staff.[4] Sadie Bell, one woman represented by the firm, told the *Times* she was raped and impregnated by a prison sergeant at Bayview Correctional Facility in Manhattan several years ago. When Bell learned she was pregnant, she was moved into solitary confinement for weeks before eventually being transferred to a different prison. There, Bell said she experienced highly painful pregnancy complications before being shackled and rushed to the hospital. Bell then learned her pregnancy was ectopic, resulting in a ruptured fallopian tube. She eventually lost five pints of blood and was left infertile by the experience. Ectopic pregnancies can result in severe complications and even death without a timely abortion.

An Alabama County Jail's War on Pregnant People

One particular U.S. county embodies the violence inflicted on incarcerated pregnant people, all detained and jailed on cruel or outright nonsensical charges to start with. At about six weeks pregnant in May 2022, a woman named Ashley Banks was arrested and jailed over an unregistered gun and possession of a small amount of marijuana. Charges of this nature will typically allow for individuals to post bond and leave jail until their trial. But when police learned Banks had smoked weed two days earlier—just before the 23-year-old learned she was pregnant—she was forced to remain in the Etowah County Detention Center in Alabama unless she entered drug rehab. But rehab centers wouldn't take Banks, who didn't qualify for addiction services offered through the state of Alabama because there was no evidence that she had a substance abuse disorder. As a result, the Alabama woman was forced to remain jailed at the Etowah County Detention Center for several months. Banks had a high-risk pregnancy because of her family's history of miscarriage and was also diagnosed with subchorionic hematoma, where blood pools near the wall of the uterus, increasing the chance of miscarriage, preterm delivery, and other complications. But because the lower bunk of her jail cell was double-booked, she was forced to sleep on the floor for weeks. Just over a month into her time in jail, Banks began bleeding and continued to bleed for five weeks, struggling with hunger and fainting spells as well.

Eventually, weeks later, a county judge released Banks from the county jail. But her case wasn't and isn't an isolated incident in the county, where AL.com reported in 2022 that as many as twelve pregnant or postpartum people suspected of drug use were held in Etowah County Detention Center in August 2022 alone. Some were jailed indefinitely without even being found guilty of any crime. Pregnancy Justice tracked over 150 "chemical endangerment" cases—cases in which pregnant people are alleged to have harmed their fetus through drug use—in Etowah County between 2010 and the summer of 2022. While just 2% of Alabama's population lives in Etowah County, it represents over 20% of pregnancy-related prosecutions in the state, which itself recorded the highest number of pregnancy-related criminal cases in the nation between 2006 and 2022. Chemical endangerment laws are meant to protect born, living children from home meth labs and substance exposure—but instead, they're weaponized by law enforcement to criminalize pregnant people, consequently endangering their health and their pregnancies.

Around the same time as Banks' experience, also in Etowah County, a mother of two named Hali Burns was arrested while visiting her newborn son in the NICU six days after giving birth in the summer of 2022 (around the *Dobbs* ruling), because she'd tested positive for methamphetamine and Subutex, a medication to treat pregnant people with opioid use disorders, during her pregnancy. Burns' lawyers said the drug tests were false positives stemming from sinus medication, and she has a prescription for Subutex. "When she first got in jail, she was right out of the hospital," Burns' partner Craig Battles told AL.com at the time. "She didn't even have panties or pads and she had just had a baby. She was stuffing paper towels or toilet paper in her pants to stop the bleeding." Burns remained in jail for months, and Battles said their young child "keeps asking what [Burns] did wrong and why she can't come home."

Burns' lawyer said that barring new moms and pregnant people from going home to await trial like all other defendants, all because of perceived threats to their fetus or newborn, is "not constitutional." For context, the lawyer added, "I have reckless murder cases where defendants have been released on bond." As a truly dystopian line of defense, the deputy district attorney for Etowah County attempted to justify the county's treatment of Burns, telling AL.com that Burns "desperately needs the help we are offering here today."

The "help" in question, of course, was jail just days after giving birth, which a maternal-fetal medicine expert told AL.com placed Burns at greater risk of a wide range of postpartum mental health problems, not to mention how the postpartum period is a critical bonding time for mothers and infants. "Separation of mothers from their infants has adverse impacts on infant and child development with ramifications that stretch into adulthood," the expert said. The year before, in 2021, another woman, Brittney Pickard, was arrested ten days after giving birth because her newborn tested positive for marijuana. Pickard said that when she learned she was going to Etowah County Detention Center, she "was still going through postpartum, still bleeding, still had stitches down there." At the jail, she said it took a day to get pads that she needed for her bleeding, and she was denied pain medication. Around that same time in 2021, another Alabama woman, not in Etowah County, was arrested and prosecuted for seeking to fill a prescription for pain medication due to debilitating back pain she was experiencing while pregnant with her sixth child.

Pickard and Burns were jailed postpartum, but others, like Banks, were arrested and jailed while still pregnant. Incarcerated pregnant people are almost twice as likely to suffer miscarriages as the general population.[5] In Alabama, pregnancy loss for alleged substance use can result in up to 99 years in prison.

Later in the fall of 2022, all within weeks of *Dobbs*, Etowah County released five women who had been jailed for alleged marijuana use and mildly updated the policy that led to some of the women's incarceration. While "chemical endangerment of a child" remains a crime, through reviewing court records, Pregnancy Justice attorney Emma Roth told me at the time that she found pregnant people who face this charge will be required to pay a $2,500 bond and fees for pretrial monitoring instead of the previously required $10,000 bond and in-patient drug treatment. The severity of that charge often resulted in pregnant people in the county being jailed indefinitely, due to lack of available beds in treatment centers. The new policy marked a small improvement, but still required pregnant people to be drug tested every 48 to 72 hours—a "ludicrous, blatantly unconstitutional" demand, Roth said, which is especially challenging for those who already have kids to take care of. Further, the new policy will still result in pretrial jailing of those who can't afford the $2,500.

"Each of these people is legally innocent. They have not been convicted of or sentenced for any crime at all, they're entitled to the presumption of innocence. But the mere fact there have been allegations leveled against them, and they're pregnant or postpartum, was sufficient for the state to feel entitled to rob them of their liberty," Roth said. "There were women we spoke to who said they had just been completely forgotten about by this system, that it was just accepted as a matter of fact that they would sit in jail for months on end, awaiting a rehab bed to open up."

One of the Etowah women Pregnancy Justice represented had been jailed for three months, despite having no diagnosis of a substance use disorder. She had just given birth seven months prior and missed her other child's fourth birthday and first day of school while jailed. Another woman was also jailed for three months, and also separated from a newborn and other young children. And another was jailed for two weeks while nine months pregnant. Her labor and contractions began during her detention.

"Not a single one of our clients is able to sleep well at night while they remain separated from their children," Roth said. "All of them have to comply with really onerous surveillance and all kinds of classes and pay fees. It's a huge, ongoing battle to be permitted to do something as fundamental and essential as parent their own children, who they miss and love more than anything."

Without *Roe*, all pregnancies are possible crime scenes. "The underlying theory behind these charges is the exact same theory that motivates abortion bans or other restrictions on bodily autonomy during pregnancy—it's the notion that when somebody becomes pregnant, their rights no longer matter, their liberty no longer matters," Roth said. "If the only concern of state actors is protecting the health and well-being of 'unborn children,' they feel entitled to trample the rights and liberty of pregnant people in the process."

Reproductive Violence and Carceral Violence

There is an extensive historical context for pregnant people's mistreatment in detention centers. Today, much of modern gynecology itself is premised on inhumane, nonconsensual research and experimentation performed on incarcerated women nearly two centuries ago.

According to the 2023 anthology *Who Would Believe a Prisoner?*, about 150 years ago, a group of Quaker women reformers in Indiana founded the country's first women's prison—a solution, they claimed, that would protect women prisoners from rape in co-ed prisons, serve as a utopia for reform that would meaningfully change incarcerated women's lives. Through landmark research conducted by incarcerated women currently or formerly held at the Indiana Women's Prison, *Who Would Believe a Prisoner?* thoroughly dismantles the feel-good fantasy of a feminist women's prison. Co-editor Elizabeth Nelson, who helped launch a college course offered at the Indiana Women's Prison to produce this research, told me that through all the women's discoveries about the prison, the "through-line is the use of different kinds of captive bodies to produce new forms of medical knowledge."

We're introduced to Dr. Theophilus Parvin, regarded by many as a founding father of the field of gynecology and obstetrics, who frequently used incarcerated women at the prison in the 1870s as test subjects. Parvin also leveraged his power to subject many to medical rape, exploiting the state's ownership of the women's bodies and studying their genitals and internal organs without their consent. Under Parvin and the Quaker reformers' care, women and girls who were perceived as sexual deviants were stripped naked, taken from their rooms, held underwater in bathtubs, and hosed down as punishment for their "disease." One incarcerated researcher, Anastazia Schmid, found that an incarcerated Black woman with uterine cancer was subjected to Parvin's experimentation, as the prison "treated" her by forcing her to continue performing hard labor, ultimately working her to her death. Parvin's research notes also include detailed instructions on how to perform abortions and end miscarriages, and Schmid suggests in *Who Would Believe a Prisoner?* that he gained this knowledge by experimenting on incarcerated women, referencing testimony from one leader of the prison that Parvin once "delivered" a stillborn fetus.

Michelle Daniel Jones, Nelson's co-editor who was incarcerated during the start of the project and is now a doctoral student at New York University in critical prison studies, told me, "Our work is a study of the medicalization of abuse at these facilities that really worked hand-in-hand with the health system—and showed how different the story is when it's written by the victims and not the dominant group." She continued, "We can't talk about the medical field today as purely altruistic, without talking about the ways it was complicit in dehumanizing captive women, who are still being mistreated today."

The medical abuse of the women held at the Indiana Women's Prison went hand in hand with sexual violence they routinely faced from prison staff, according to testimony that Schmid and other incarcerated scholars uncovered through their archival research. One woman, Eva, was infected with syphilis after repeatedly being raped by a steward at the prison. She tried to sue the prison but was dismissed because of her status. The book is named after her experience: "You can't believe that woman. I've caught her in a thousand lies," the warden, who represented the steward in court, said of Eva. This appraisal held in court, and the steward faced no consequences. His quote, Jones said, encapsulates the conditions uncovered in *Who Would Believe a Prisoner?* Incarcerated women were treated not just as uncredible and subhuman—their consent was also irrelevant, whether for sexual encounters or medical experimentation.

Our modern medical system continues to disregard the pain and discomfort of women and pregnant people, feeding alarmingly high maternal mortality rates, when their complaints and concerns are ignored by hospitals. Pregnant people in prisons are an innately high-risk maternal health group, Jones stressed. And abusive medical practices and the total policing of incarcerated women's sexual and reproductive lives have only persisted. Between 2006 and 2010, doctors reportedly performed nonconsensual sterilizations on 148 incarcerated women at a California prison.[6] A whistleblower at an ICE facility claimed in 2020 that doctors allegedly performed mass, forced sterilizations on detained immigrant women. Given the demographics of women's prisons, populated disproportionately by Black women, women of color, and poor people, Jones recognizes this targeted practice as an ongoing form of eugenics.

There are currently 29 federal women's prisons, and about 10% of all incarcerated people are women. The Indiana Women's Prison stands to this day as a maximum-security facility that boasts of its capacity to imprison over 700 women.

Chapter 7

The Medicalization of Abuse

In 2024, the Supreme Court ruled that doctors in Idaho could provide pregnant people with emergency abortion care without fear of prosecution. But they didn't offer a definitive ruling on whether pregnant people experiencing complications have a federal right to receive this emergency care—they ultimately sent the case down to a lower court, deliberately leaving the door open for continued lawsuits and legal chaos. The ruling, *Moyle v. United States*, offered Idaho doctors some protections, albeit temporary pending additional litigation. But still, the damage to the state's maternal care infrastructure, particularly in rural parts of the state, was done: By then, large swaths of Idaho OB-GYNs fled out of fear that simply doing their jobs could result in prison time. "Idaho provides a terrifying cautionary tale for our nation," Idaho's Democratic party Chair Lauren Necochea said after the *Moyle* ruling. "Our small state has lost nearly a quarter of our OB-GYNs, over half our maternal and fetal medicine specialists, and three labor and delivery wards."

A report from earlier that year showed about 22% of OB-GYNs in Idaho stopped practicing after the abortion ban took effect in 2022.[1] Also in the days after the *Moyle* ruling, Dr. Caitlin Gustafson, president of the Idaho Coalition for Safe Healthcare and a family physician who's practiced in rural parts of the state for over 20 years, described Idaho's health care system as being "in crisis." Retaining health care workers within a punishing legal landscape that's inherently at odds with their ability to do their jobs is an all but impossible task. Within the first months of 2024, Luke's Medical Center in Boise had to transfer six patients in need of emergency abortions to out-of-state hospitals via helicopter.

In March 2023, the first hospital based in a rural part of Idaho announced that it had shuttered its labor and delivery department, after almost all its staff left out of fear of being prosecuted for offering pregnancy-related care that could be construed as abortion. "The Idaho Legislature continues to pass bills that criminalize physicians for medical care nationally recognized as the standard of care. Consequences for Idaho physicians providing the standard of care may include civil litigation and criminal prosecution, leading to jail time or fines," a press release for the hospital said. In June 2024, the president of the Idaho Hospital Association told Northwest Public Broadcasting that "several of our members are struggling to hire OBGYNs" as well as maternal fetal medicine doctors. "Those searches are going sometimes six months, eight months, even up to a year before they can find somebody that's willing to come and practice that kind of medicine."

This—maternal care deserts that will endanger pregnant people's lives—is a long-term issue: One survey from 2024 found U.S. medical students are less likely to apply to residency programs in states with abortion bans.[2] A survey from 2023 showed three out of four future U.S. doctors said abortion bans are a major factor in where they'll apply for residencies. Such is the impact of abortion bans: the shuttering of access to basic health care inevitably enacts horrific violence on pregnant patients, with disparate impacts on communities already marginalized by the health system—that is, people of color, poor people, and certainly, domestic violence victims. As previously noted, 32% of respondents to a 2024 survey of domestic violence victims said they lack access to a medical professional who focuses on reproductive health or pregnancy. Again, as the National Domestic Violence Hotline's Mariam Durrani told me, "the risk rises" when victims don't have access to this sometimes life-saving care, which the Hotline survey respondents called a "lifeline." Many victims are now losing that lifeline.

It didn't help that, as health care providers awaited further litigation around *Moyle*, anti-abortion "researchers" set to work to further endanger pregnant people with pseudoscience—namely, they pushed the lie that there's no medical need for emergency abortions. In a July 2024 paper in Medical Research Archives, James Studnicki and OB-GYN Dr. Ingrid Skop of the anti-abortion Charlotte Lozier Institute claimed that, in lieu of emergency abortions, doctors should perform C-sections to end dangerous pregnancies, even though C-sections are far riskier and more invasive. These are the same researchers who submitted a since-retracted "study" lying that medication abortion is unsafe, cited in a different Supreme Court case that unsuccessfully tried to further-restrict medication abortion. "[M]any physicians argue that it is almost never necessary to end the life of a child directly and intentionally by an abortion procedure," they wrote. "[W]hen a pregnancy endangering the life of the mother requires termination, a direct 'dismemberment' dilation and evacuation (D&E) abortion may be unnecessary, as delivery can usually be performed with a standard obstetric intervention such as labor induction or cesarean section." One OB-GYN responded to this in an interview with *States Newsroom*, calling C-sections "far more complicated," "dangerous," and confusing than abortion—all for "the same end goal" to end a nonviable, unsafe pregnancy.[3] C-sections also come with greater risk of hemorrhaging, impaired future fertility, and other complications than abortion does.

Per *States Newsroom*, several states that have banned abortion and threaten doctors with prison time have already seen a rise in C-sections instead of emergency abortions as a treatment for dangerous pregnancies. This is meant to circumvent legal risk, but it comes at the expense of patient safety. A 2024 report from Physicians for Human Rights and other organizations interviewed dozens of doctors in Louisiana (where an abortion ban threatens abortion providers with up to 15 years in prison and $200,000 in fines) and found a sharp rise in C-sections over emergency abortions.[4] One researcher told NPR she'd heard from a doctor who said they did this "to preserve the appearance of not doing an abortion."

"There are going to be deaths that didn't have to happen. There are going to be severe complications that didn't have to happen," a doctor cautions in the PRH report. It's state-sanctioned medical abuse at its most abhorrent.

And there are layers to this abuse.

The medical system, fraught with medical racism and disparate harm for already marginalized patients, is also physically dangerous for survivors and pregnant people: Alarmingly, reporting in recent years has shown endemic medical rape and lack of trauma-informed care that exposes victims to frequent retraumatization, with pregnant people shown to be more vulnerable. Abortion bans make all of this worse.

Pregnant Women Interrogated in Their Hospital Beds

In May 2023, eight more women joined the *Zurawski* lawsuit against the state of Texas to clarify when someone can receive emergency, potentially life-saving abortion. All the women said ambiguities in the state's ban placed their lives at risk as they experienced life-threatening pregnancy complications. One of those eight women was Kiersten Hogan, a survivor of domestic violence who recounted a particularly haunting story of being held for five days against her will at a religious hospital so she wouldn't be able to leave and get the emergency abortion she needed. Hogan's detainment was part of an alarming phenomenon in this country. Hospitals, including non-religious hospitals, have a history of holding pregnant people experiencing complications against their will, performing unwanted procedures on them, or even colluding with law enforcement to have them detained. Hogan's case preceded *Dobbs*, a consequence of Texas' 2021 S.B. 8 abortion ban, as well as the dangerous overreach of religious hospitals. But post-*Dobbs*, as abortion bans across the country threaten to jail or punish doctors who provide abortion, there's even greater risk of cases like Hogan's.

"What's scary is that it doesn't have to be an anti-abortion idealogue, religious hospital," If/When/How's Farah Diaz-Tello told me in 2023. When hospitals misinterpret abortion laws, as they fear they'll be held liable if a patient leaves their care and has an abortion elsewhere, they're more likely to police their patients' behaviors—including by detaining or reporting them to law enforcement. "Those fears are totally misplaced and misguided. But the one suffering, as a result, is the patient."

"Texas law caused me to be . . . detained against my will for five days and treated like a criminal all during the most traumatic and heartbreaking experience I've had in my life to date," Hogan said in 2023. She recounted being forced to remain in the hospital until she gave birth to a stillborn fetus, constantly monitored and afraid to so much as leave her room to use the restroom. Lynn Paltrow, the founder of Pregnancy Justice, told me in 2023 that she'd worked on and was familiar with numerous, similar cases to Hogan's over the years—including cases in which women and pregnant people were jailed specifically to prevent them from having abortions or "harming" their fetuses. Brittany Watts of Ohio filed a lawsuit in 2025 claiming that police interrogated her in her hospital bed, all while she was "tethered" to the bed "with IVs." Her suit alleges that two different nurses and a police officer "knowingly" conspired to "fabricate evidence to falsely implicate" Watts in criminal conduct.

In 2013, before arresting and jailing her, police interrogated Purvi Patel in her hospital bed over her stillbirth and alleged abortion. That same year, an Oklahoma woman who sought medical care for her pregnancy complications was reported by hospital workers to police for being "noncompliant." She was arrested and died in jail days later due to complications from an ectopic pregnancy. In 2009, a Florida woman was held against her will at a hospital that obtained a court order to keep her in its charge after the hospital learned she was at risk of miscarriage. There, she was forced to undergo an unwanted cesarean procedure, per Pregnancy Justice's tracking.

This collusion between law enforcement and the medical system to enact state violence upon pregnant people isn't out of the ordinary. Again, the majority of cases of pregnancy criminalization come to the attention of police only after patients are reported by health care workers, consequently convincing many pregnant people that it's unsafe to seek out medical care at all.

Paltrow told me that hospitals have no obligation or right to hold patients against their will and, to the contrary, such a practice is illegal. Because so many hospitals are overly cautious or outright misinformed about the extent of their liability under abortion bans, they take advantage of patients being "easily intimidated by doctors and hospital staff" and the sharply unequal doctor-patient power dynamic, Paltrow said. Sometimes, she added, insurance coverage is even used as leverage against patients, who are told—incorrectly—that a service or procedure won't be covered if they leave the hospital against medical advice.

When *Roe* fell, this "opened doors for states to create further restrictions on pregnant people in the name of fetal rights," Diaz-Tello told me, and to "determine the care or freedoms someone has based on the effects it might have on the fetus." That threat of fetal personhood only renders pregnant people more vulnerable to possible detainment by hospitals on top of significant legal troubles. Abortion bans encourage and all but pressure hospitals and law enforcement agencies to prioritize protecting a fetus—even if this means terrorizing and effectively holding pregnant people captive. The impacts on patients who experience this mistreatment can be significant: Hogan, a survivor who fled an abusive relationship upon becoming pregnant, testified in 2023 that she's being treated for PTSD as a direct result of her traumatic isolation at the Texas religious hospital. She escaped one abuser for another: the state, and the medical system under state laws. And despite stories like hers, still, no policies exist requiring patients to be informed of their rights to leave medical facilities, whether they're pregnant or not.

An Invasive Medical System

In some ways, abuse and sexual assault are baked into the very medical services that pregnant and pregnant-capable patients receive. Consider, again, Kentucky's law which requires abortion seekers to have an invasive, transvaginal ultrasound before they can have the procedure. Several states have similar such laws. In 2013, one article in the *Journal of Criminal Law and Criminology* compiles perspectives from doctors, lawmakers, and rape victims assessing state-mandated pre-abortion ultrasounds as rape:

> A doctor reacted to this kind of legislation by saying, "I do not feel that it is reactionary or even inaccurate to describe an unwanted, non-indicated transvaginal ultrasound as 'rape.' If I insert ANY object into ANY orifice without informed consent, it is rape. And coercion of any kind negates consent, informed or otherwise." A Virginia state legislator considering such a bill said, "What's before us is akin to rape." A rape victim expressed her thoughts in a recent blog post: "I have been a victim of rape, so I don't use the word lightly, but there's no other way to put it." Political commentator Rachel Maddow characterized the 2012 Virginia law as "a physical penetration of the body . . . by state order, without your consent. That would be forced on you as a condition of your being allowed to have an abortion . . ." An Alabama state senator said: "If you look up the term rape, that's what it is: the penetration of the vagina without the woman's consent."[5]

This is sexual violence. Texas reproductive and survivor justice activist, Maleeha Aziz, described her 2013 visit to an anti-abortion crisis pregnancy center, which required her to have an ultrasound, as tantamount to sexual violence. "Had I known that was a fake clinic all those years ago, would I let them touch me? Absolutely not. I wouldn't have even gone in there. I was deceived and violated," she told me in 2024. In 2023, the CDC released the findings of a survey which showed one in five women experienced mistreatment while receiving medical care for their most recent pregnancy. Respondents reported being verbally abused, having requests for help go unanswered, and, chillingly, having their physical privacy infringed upon, among other forms of mistreatment. Obstetric violence isn't uncommon: Speaking to the anti-sexual violence advocacy organization RAINN, a woman named Marissa Hoechstetter shared that she was repeatedly sexually assaulted by the OB-GYN she saw during her pregnancy. "With medical professionals, there's often a legitimate reason for why their hands are on your body. There's a gray area and the minute you step into their office, they have power over you," Hoechstetter said. "Looking back, there were a lot of things that felt odd, but I was pregnant and focused on my babies."

Hoechstetter eventually connected with other survivors victimized by the same hospital. In 2023, over 300 patients of Robert Hadden, a former Columbia gynecologist who was convicted of sexual abuse, came forward as victims of his. Data from the U.S. National Practitioner Data Bank indicates that between 2003 and 2013, 862 physicians faced state licensing disciplinary actions due to 974 cases of sexual misconduct. One survey from the 1990s found nearly 10% of physicians report having engaged in sexual contact with at least one patient,[6] which legal experts have characterized as innately "suspect" due to the power dynamics of a doctor-patient relationship.[7]

But in addition to stories like Hoechstetter's, in some ways, obstetric violence is embedded in the medical system writ large, including the policies that both govern and fail to govern it. In 2023, several states passed laws against nonconsensual pelvic exams, and a year later in 2024, the Biden administration's Health and Human Services Department explicitly stated that teaching hospitals can no longer allow this practice.[8]

The Hastings Center has estimated as many as 3.6 million U.S. adults may have received a pelvic exam or other intimate exams without their consent between 2018 and 2023.[9] Only about half of states currently have laws requiring consent for pelvic exams while patients are unconscious, according to a review by the American Journal of Law & Medicine published in November 2022.[10] Since that review, several states including, in 2023, Missouri, Montana, and Colorado, have also banned nonconsensual pelvic exams. California became the first to pass such a law in 2003. Still, activist and filmmaker A'magine Goddard— whose documentary, At Your Cervix, exposes pervasive violations of consent in gynecology—has raised concerns about the specifics of these new state laws. She told me in 2024 that these laws sometimes fail to carve out "a clear opportunity" for patients to opt out of these exams. In 2005, 75% of surveyed medical students at the University of Oklahoma self-reported performing pelvic exams on patients who couldn't consent, including unconscious patients.

Goddard told me she's spoken to several survivors of nonconsensual pelvic exams and other sexual abuse from health care providers and heard from them firsthand about how PTSD continues to manifest in their day-to-day lives. "It takes a tremendous toll, and in the bigger picture, it makes them afraid to seek health care or go to the doctor because trust is so eroded between patient and provider, where their future health is affected," Goddard said. "They're afraid to get health care they need because of what's happened to them. It's a very long-term problem." Consequently, experiencing such a violation, she explained, can impact survivors' health and well-being for years to come for the rest of their lives.

Sexual violence, which all too often impacts those seeking sexual and reproductive health services, presents a looming threat to all patients—and that's inseparable from the violence now wrought by abortion bans. All of it is connected: the systemic disregard for bodily autonomy, the discouragement of pregnant and pregnant-capable people from seeking essential health care, and the state-mandated violence that belies all of this.

Chapter 8

The Mythology of Rape Exceptions

Shortly after Election Day in 2024, Donald Trump unsuccessfully attempted to appoint former Congressman Matt Gaetz to run the Justice Department—an agency that could potentially establish a federal abortion ban by wielding the Comstock Act of 1873, a law that could prohibit the mailing of abortion pills or abortion-related medical supplies as "obscene materials." But Gaetz's nomination was thrown into chaos by allegations that he'd sex trafficked a minor. Elon Musk, Trump's billionaire adviser who has sexual misconduct allegations himself, said the allegations against Gaetz were "worth less than nothing . . . a man is considered innocent until proven guilty." Ironically, Musk made this argument despite continuing to support Trump, who a jury found civilly liable for sexual abuse in 2023. As always, "innocent until proven guilty" is just a slogan to men like Musk because there's no proof of guilt they'll really accept. Time and again, when victims come forward, whether they have only their testimony or an arsenal of evidence, they're discredited, turned away, even punished—because gender-based violence is normative in our society, because beneath surface-level condemnation, our society does not regard gender-based violence as morally wrong. In 2022, when a North Carolina Republican called for a "community-level review process" for rape victims to seek abortions under abortion bans, this is the context that his smug, cruel proposal ignored: Gender-based violations are impossible to "prove" in a fundamentally misogynistic society that does not recognize even the most egregious behaviors—like, say, forced pregnancy—as violent toward women and victims. This is why, despite the outsized attention that rape exceptions receive in advocacy spaces and political debates, we should regard exceptions with skepticism.

In the summer of 2023, we learned the story of a 13-year-old girl in Mississippi who found herself forced to balance the seventh grade with raising her newborn baby. The girl learned she was pregnant after being raped and was unable to access abortion care due to Mississippi's ban, which took effect in June 2022. The girl's mother said the family was unaware the state's abortion ban offered a rape exception, and the family couldn't afford to travel to Chicago, which is the nearest place where abortion is legal. They were left without any options.

According to a 2024 report about the family from ABC News, despite the Mississippi ban's stated exception for rape, there were just four abortions in the state in all of 2023 (compared to 3,800 in 2021), suggesting the exception is all but inaccessible. After all, we know that rape-induced pregnancies aren't an anomaly; researchers have estimated that tens of thousands occurred in states that had banned abortion during the year after *Dobbs* alone—including Mississippi.[1]

In addition to lack of awareness about the varying clauses of Mississippi's abortion law, there's complete lack of direction or guidance about how to seek the rape exception: In 2023, *Time* contacted the state attorney general's office, the state Board of Medical Licensure, and the state Medical Association seeking information about how to invoke the rape exception and didn't receive a response. The 13-year-old's family reported her rape to the police and it took a full year for police to make an arrest in her case. Despite that police report, the child was still unable to receive an abortion.

According to experts who spoke to ABC, even if the child's family had known they could seek abortion care under the law's rape exception, it's unlikely they would have found a health care provider willing to offer the procedure in the state given the legal risks. Many abortion providers have left Mississippi since the ban took effect. "If I couldn't figure out how to get a rape exception, how could this girl and her family?" *Time*'s Charlotte Alter wrote in her 2023 report telling the 13-year-old's story.

Alina Salganicoff, senior vice president and director of Women's Health Policy at Kaiser Family Foundation, told ABC that due to abortion bans, many health care providers are too afraid to help patients, even rape victims:

> Physicians have so much at stake in terms of losing their medical license, financial penalties, and, in some cases, criminalization leading to jail time. So it is very concerning for them to take the risk of performing an abortion unless they are absolutely certain that they won't be penalized for this.

Jessica Tarleton, an obstetrician in South Carolina, told NPR in 2024 that aspects of the rape exception attached to South Carolina's abortion ban cause her and patients to feel like "potential criminals," as doctors are required to report abortions performed under the exception to law enforcement. "Somebody comes into the emergency room who's been shot, we don't ask them what they did to be in a position to be shot. We take care of the patient."

Idaho's abortion ban requires victims to produce a police report for medical providers in order to qualify for a rape exception. But this puts them in a logistically impossible situation: As victim advocates in the state pointed out in 2022, police departments don't release reports until a case is closed, preventing victims from receiving timely abortion care. The Idaho legislature consequently made an amendment requiring police departments to produce a report within 72 hours, but NPR reported there's no indicator that police departments are adhering to this requirement.[2]

I'm reminded of Center for Reproductive Rights attorney Linda Goldstein's words to me in 2024, asserting that exceptions attached to abortion bans "don't work—that's really the bottom line," and calling exceptions, like Mississippi's rape exception, "window-dressing to make abortion bans look reasonable."

Rape exceptions largely hinge on respectability politics. They separate "good" abortions from "bad," frivolous abortions, and exist to give abortion laws a veneer of compassion while purposefully failing to help victims in practice. Many state abortion bans are criticized for lacking rape exceptions. But laws that include such exceptions carry all the same implicit violence. As the available data in Mississippi suggests, few rape victims seeking abortion care successfully access or even know how to seek out the exception. Many abortion restrictions, even from before *Dobbs*, have required victims to report their rape to the police or receive medical clearance for the exception, all within health and legal systems that have proven hostile to them. In 2023, one Tennessee bill nearly added a rape exception to the state's total abortion ban that would threaten those who "lied" about being raped to access care with three years in prison. This addendum was ultimately struck, not because it was both absurd and violent, but because Tennessee lawmakers killed the bill to prevent the addition of a rape exception altogether.

The following year, Missouri Republicans blocked a bill to add a rape exception to their own abortion ban. One explained his vote by arguing that being forced to carry their rapist's baby could be "healing" for victims; another inexplicably argued that under the exception, "a one-year-old could get an abortion." In May 2024, Louisiana Republicans blocked a rape exception, too. One argued teenagers would simply lie about being raped—all while an OB-GYN testified before the legislature that she and her colleagues have had to deliver babies to teens as young as 13. And in January 2025, an Indiana lawmaker introduced a bill that, in addition to criminalizing possession of abortion pills, required rape victims to submit legal affidavits to access abortion, threatening them with perjury for supposed false reports.[3] At the same time as the Indiana bill, a New Hampshire Republican introduced a 15-week abortion ban and said the bill would require that rape be reported within a short period to access an exception, so the exception couldn't be used as a "convenient excuse."

In effect, rape exceptions are "entirely disingenuous," Destini Spaeth, an organizer at the North Dakota-based Prairie Abortion Fund (formerly the Women In Need abortion fund), told me in 2023, referencing the Tennessee bill. They're merely "PR for anti-abortion politicians" while serving as a "deterrent" to survivors. Spaeth's group is dedicated to serving survivors' reproductive care needs. "[Rape exceptions are] just another round of violation of their autonomy within the health care system, within a police and judicial system that routinely hurts survivors." Tennessee's bill was built on existing, systemic barriers: Sexual assault survivors are often threatened with criminalization, sometimes upon reporting their assailant, and face jarringly high rates of incarceration. And criminal charges for pregnancy outcomes—including abortion—often implicate victims of violence: As previously mentioned in 2019, Alabama resident Marshae Jones was jailed for fetal homicide when she miscarried after she was shot.

Exceptions, survivor and reproductive justice activist Alison Turkos told me in 2022, have allowed "survivors' trauma to be reduced to currency, and measured with a yardstick to see if you can get an abortion."

The Anti-Abortion Movement Is No Longer Trying to Hide

Anti-abortion politicians have long been emphatic about one thing: Abortion is murder. Still, for years, this "logic" hasn't held up against their occasional concession that abortion bans should make exceptions for rape. In recent years, both in the months leading up to *Dobbs* and after the ruling, this dynamic has shifted dramatically. In 2022, a wave of new abortion restrictions lacked rape exceptions. Florida's legislature voted to reject adding an exception to its 15-week abortion ban. Lawmakers in Arizona and West Virginia did the same to their own 15-week bans. In 2021, Texas' S.B. 8 memorably lacked a rape exception, and Gov. Greg Abbott justified this by insisting he'd invest more in policing to "eliminate" rapists. It's a relatively recent development that politicians have been saying the quiet part out loud. Over a decade ago, then-Missouri Senate candidate Todd Akin tanked his campaign by asserting that we don't need rape exceptions to abortion bans because "legitimate rape" can't lead to pregnancy. Richard Mourdock sank his own bid for Senate in Indiana in a similar way that same year, saying that when a woman becomes pregnant from rape, "God intended" that. Comments like this, today, would be fairly run-of-the-mill. Weeks before the 2024 election, one Texas state legislature candidate said he wouldn't let his daughter have an abortion if she were raped: "If I had a daughter, and that would have been a rape, I think I would say, no, we're going to have the baby." A Michigan Republican candidate said in 2022 that he once told his daughters, "If rape is inevitable, you should just lie back and enjoy it." That same year, an Ohio Republican in the state legislature called pregnancy from rape "an opportunity," while a Utah lawmaker suggested rape-induced pregnancies don't actually happen because women can "control that intake of semen."

In 2017, Alison Turkos survived being kidnapped and gang-raped on a Lyft ride in New York. The experience changed the course of her life: For nearly a decade before the assault by her Lyft driver, Turkos had been working in the reproductive justice movement, advocating for pregnant people's bodily autonomy. In the years since her assault, she's become a leader in organizing at the intersections of survivor and reproductive justice. Turkos told me in 2022 that she believes anti-abortion lawmakers are increasingly abandoning their performance of support for victims and "showing their true colors," because they've already "been able to get so far." Lawmakers have passed hundreds of bans and restrictions in the last decade by "using survivors as a shield while trying to fast-track these bills through the legislature." In other words, by including rape exceptions and therefore permitting abortions for the "right reasons," legislators could shut down criticisms of their bills as cruel or anti-women. Through all of this success, they eventually realized they didn't even need these exceptions.

On a cultural level, rape exceptions have implicitly fueled the misconception that rape is easy for victims to "prove" to law enforcement or other authorities, brushing away the retraumatizing process of reporting rape as a footnote in a survivor's path to getting an abortion. Cazembe Murphy Jackson, a Black trans man, shared his story of being raped by a group of four men in a small town in Texas in 2019 prior to transitioning. He learned he was pregnant six weeks later. He was able to "scrape together the funds" to have the abortion, and had reported his rape to the police, although he said he felt "dismissed" by them. But his experience still showed him that rape exceptions fail to support "those of us who don't call the police, because the police are often not helpful, particularly to survivors from communities of color," he wrote.[4]

In 2019, Texas state Rep. Donna Howard authored a bill that created a first-in-the-nation Sexual Assault Survivors Task Force in the Governor's Office to collect information on how government agencies respond to sexual assault reports and develop survivor-centric best practices. Howard told me in 2022 that she was baffled by Abbott's bizarre promise to simply "end rape" in defense of S.B. 8—particularly his claim that he could do so by "getting rapists off the street," despite how most cases of sexual violence are perpetrated by non-strangers and intimate partners. Even when abortion laws have included exceptions for rape, Howard stressed that they reflect the carceral, "law and order" politics of Abbott's pledge to end rape, as these exceptions can amount to a dangerous form of mandatory reporting that denies survivors agency. This can even force pregnant survivors to be implicated in the criminal legal system against their will.

In 2022, Florida Republicans described their proposed 15-week ban, which lacked a rape exception, as "generous" to pregnant people. Since, the state has enacted a six-week abortion ban. In 2024, a ballot measure to restore the right to abortion received a decisive 57% of the vote but didn't reach the state's 60% requirement and failed. State Sen. Lauren Book, a survivor of child sexual abuse, told me in 2022 that the lack of a rape exception amounts to "basically putting a gun to a pregnant survivor's head with these laws—it's the state further taking control of a woman, of their power and control, just like the rapist, really."

The Uphill Battle for Exceptions

In the summer of 2022, after the Supreme Court overturned *Roe*, Hadley Duvall wrote a Facebook post about her experience becoming pregnant after her stepfather raped her when she was twelve years old. Duvall, now an adult, eventually miscarried the rape-induced pregnancy. That was the first time she publicly shared her story, she told me in 2024, because she wanted people in her community in Kentucky to understand the implications of *Dobbs* for survivors like her. A year after she shared her story, Democratic Kentucky Gov. Andy Beshear, who was running for reelection, reached out to Duvall, inviting her to film an ad for his campaign. In the ad, which ran in September 2023, Duvall addressed Beshear's Republican, anti-abortion rival, state Attorney General Daniel Cameron, directly: "This is to you, Daniel Cameron. To tell a 12-year-old girl she must have the baby of her stepfather who raped her is unthinkable. I'm speaking out because women and girls need to have options. Daniel Cameron would give us none."

Thanks to Duvall's ad, in the weeks leading up to the election, Cameron was forced to go on the defensive for his flip-flopping on whether he supported rape exceptions to abortion bans. In November 2023, Beshear won the election handily in the deep-red state.

And in January 2024, Duvall worked quickly: She joined state Sen. David Yates as he filed a bill to add exceptions to Kentucky's total abortion ban. Beshear immediately promised to sign it. A rape-induced pregnancy just compounds "the trauma and anxiety you're already struggling to recover from every single day after being assaulted," Hadley told me. "For you to be forced to carry that pregnancy, have your rape always be with you, be powerless over your own body from not only a violent sexual act but now being forced to give birth—why would we do that to women?"

At the intersections of reproductive and survivor justice, and in a deeply conservative political environment, Hadley's activism is powerful and important. Still, elsewhere, previous attempts to get rape exceptions added to the abortion bans of states like Tennessee have been roundly defeated. All efforts in Tennessee have been shot down by anti-abortion Republicans in the legislature since 2022. In Florida, a six-week ban that Gov. Ron DeSantis (R) signed in 2023 offered a narrow rape exception for those who could supply adequate "proof" of their rape, including a "restraining order, police report, medical record, or other court order or documentation" to "verify" they were raped. This prompted fierce protest from survivors and activists who testified against the bill in the state Capitol, accusing lawmakers of "forcibly [putting] someone through a second rape." Lawmakers refused to listen.

Within a month of Beshear's victory, in December 2023, a woman in Kentucky sued the state for no other reason than that she simply did not want to be pregnant. The lawsuit was ultimately withdrawn after the plaintiff learned her embryo no longer had cardiac activity, and Kentucky's total ban remains active. But on principle, the lawsuit made an important point: Abortion should be available to anyone who seeks it for any reason, without forcing them to prove anything or endure any sexual or medical trauma.

Violence against Children

Something else Duvall said stood out to me: If "Hadley's law" passed, she stressed that many rape victims who seek care under the exception will be "younger," like she was, and "their bodies can't go through these things." She continued, "Being forced to carry a nonviable pregnancy to full term is traumatic. Knowing that carrying a baby is detrimental to your health but may not immediately fall in the category of life-threatening, so you're forced to carry it, is traumatic."

Anyone should be able to get an abortion for any reason. That truth coexists with the disproportionality of who is harmed the most by abortion bans—namely underage rape victims, like the ten-year-old Ohio girl who was forced to travel to Indiana for abortion care in July 2022, just days after *Dobbs*, or the (at least) 105 minors who had to leave Texas for abortion care in 2023, six of whom were child abuse victims under 12. These are the children who are erased or, worse, dehumanized, by extremists like Dr. Ingrid Skop, the anti-abortion doctor mentioned earlier who was appointed to Texas' Maternal Mortality Committee in 2024, despite or perhaps because she cruelly testified before Congress that child rape victims as young as nine or ten years old can safely carry a pregnancy.

The Mississippi child rape victim's family told ABC News in 2024 that they're still processing the child's rape, all while trying to raise a baby, living in one of the poorest counties in the state. In 2023, the girl's mother recounted being treated dismissively by the local police department before an arrest was eventually made. Initially, when the child's pregnancy was first discovered at the emergency room, her mother told *Time* that a nurse asked the girl, "What have you been doing?" implying the pregnancy was the child's fault. The family would later be forced to fund-raise so they could move houses in order "to relocate away from the rapist and closer to family so that Ashley [a pseudonym for the child] can get a fresh start," they wrote in a GoFundMe page in 2023.

COERCION

This is the violence wrought by abortion bans, disproportion-ately inflicted on the most vulnerable victims of abuse—and there is no circumventing or minimizing this harm through the window-dressing of exceptions. "Protecting survivors means no abortion bans, not just exceptions that don't work," Prairie Fund's Destini Spaeth tells me.

Chapter 9

How Liberalism Abandoned Reproductive Justice

In June 2022, *Dobbs* capitalized on years of inaction and concessions from liberal politicians, and the consequent hollowing of reproductive rights across the country. *Dobbs* made everything immeasurably worse, but it's by no means the only source of present-day suffering for women, pregnant people, and survivors in this country.

Roe was never enough, leaving holes and significant vulnerabilities where abortion could be restricted, and pregnancy policed. As we chart our path forward, *Roe* shouldn't be our policy aspiration. Nor should it be dangled over our heads like a carrot by politicians each election cycle, as they insist on our donations and unquestioning support so they might restore our rights, which they lost for us in the first place. In the months leading up to the 2024 presidential election, Democratic leaders campaigned heavily on the threat of a Republican president—Donald Trump—enacting Project 2025, a 900-page policy agenda created by the far-right Heritage Foundation, detailing how the executive branch could bypass Congress to impose a national abortion ban, ban pornography, and terrorize LGBTQ people, among other horrific objectives.[1] Project 2025 made for a terrifying boogeyman, but arguably even more concerning was top Democrats' lack of their own version of Project 2025, a vision for how a Democratic president could restore abortion rights and protect pregnant and queer people to the fullest extent via their administration. Democrats' lack of vision cost them the election—and, consequently, large swaths of the population lost further rights and protections.

In 1969, in the years before the Supreme Court originally decided *Roe*, activists formed an organization called NARAL— the National Association for the Repeal of Abortion Laws. (The organization has since renamed itself Reproductive Freedom for All.) Renee Bracey Sherman, founder and executive director of We Testify, an organization that helps people tell their abortion stories to promote cultural change, told Jezebel in 2023: "That is what our movement originally asked for, because then it is actually up to the person who needs the abortion and the skill of their provider—the midwife, nurse, whoever's in the community willing to provide." And, to be clear, despite the recurring mainstream media narrative that the country is evenly split on the supposedly controversial issue of abortion, 81% of voters said in 2024 that they don't believe the government should interfere with our pregnancies, period.[2] (Polling results are largely shaped by how questions are framed—if we ask *whether* the government should legislate around our bodies and pregnancies, and not *when* in a pregnancy the government should intervene, answers will likely vary.)

Roe didn't repeal abortion laws; it created a right to abortion. But it also set the terms for abortion to be policed, leaving open the door for laws to establish arbitrary legal cut-offs for abortion, and allow funding restrictions and TRAP laws that decimate meaningful access to abortion. That's why the repeal of abortion laws—that is, ending state intervention and policing of pregnancies—should be our movement's ultimate and clearly stated objective.

But since *Dobbs*, Democratic politicians who have historically been largely unhelpful on the issues of abortion and reproductive justice have insisted on our votes to "save *Roe*"—and nothing more. The restoration of *Roe* became the immediate slogan of President Biden's reelection campaign post-*Dobbs*, without elaborating on what real steps would be taken to help people living under abortion bans *right now*. The slogan also carried dark irony while the administration fueled horrific reproductive violence abroad with our taxes.

In October 2023, when Israel escalated its decades-long genocide against Palestinians and waged a brutal campaign of bombardment and starvation on Gaza, the Biden administration consistently funded, armed, and offered Israel political cover and legitimacy. By the summer of 2024, research published by Lancet Journal estimated that nearly 186,000 Palestinians in Gaza had been killed within under a year. Women and children comprised 70% of the casualties.[3] And pregnant people, menstruating people, and particularly children suffered from the dearth of reproductive care. The miscarriage rate soared 300%, one humanitarian agency told me in the winter of 2024; later that year, the organization Medical Aid for Palestinians reported the maternal mortality rate had increased 20% since October, and the infant mortality rate had increased 15%.[4] Emergency C-sections were routinely performed without anesthetic, resulting in excruciating pain and often leading to deadly infections.[5] Hospitals and the medical system were entirely overwhelmed, directly targeted by the Israeli military, as a result of both Israel's siege on Gaza and its deliberate attacks on hospitals and aid workers; consequently, there were no clean or safe places to give birth, or to recover and take shelter after giving birth. Infections and both maternal and infant mortality soared, humanitarian agencies said. A complete lack of clean water and food hit nursing mothers and newborns the hardest. Humanitarian agencies reported that sexual violence perpetrated by Israeli soldiers against Palestinian men, women, and children was rampant—a tragic inevitability amid colonial aggression, as sexual violence is a timeless tool of colonization.

And the violence was entirely manmade—by Israel and the U.S. under President Biden. At least twice, Biden bypassed Congress to send additional bombs and weapons to Israel.

In January 2024, as the rampant atrocities against pregnant Palestinian women persisted, the day after the 51st anniversary of the *Roe* ruling, President Biden and Vice President Kamala Harris held a campaign rally centering their support for reproductive rights. The "Reproductive Freedom Campaign Rally" featured a stage decorated with signs that read "Defend Choice" and "Restore *Roe*." After being introduced by Amanda Zurawski, the lead plaintiff in the Texas lawsuit filed by women denied emergency abortions, Biden was interrupted by protesters 14 times. They weren't there to criticize Biden's abortion rights position (which, frankly, did leave a lot to be desired), but rather, the administration's support for Israel's genocide against Gaza.

"When we support reproductive rights and justice, we can't exclude the women of Gaza from that analysis," Danaka Katovich, one of the protest organizers, told me at the time. At that point, the Gaza Health Ministry estimated over 25,000 Palestinians had been killed by Israel since October 2023. Protesters at the Biden-Harris event chanted "Genocide Joe" and asked Biden "how many babies have you killed today?" One protester told me that as she was taken away, Biden pointed at and called her a Trump supporter.

The "Restore *Roe*" rally was co-organized by national reproductive and women's rights groups including the National Organization for Women (NOW), Reproductive Freedom for All (formerly NARAL), Planned Parenthood and its Virginia affiliate, and REPRO Rising Virginia. All these organizations had faced significant pressure from others in the reproductive rights and justice movements over their continued public support for the Biden administration, despite its proactive role in the extensively documented suffering of pregnant people in Gaza.

"We're not going to . . . allow them to sanitize the reality of what they're supporting," Hazami Barmada, the Palestinian-American activist who Biden called a Trump supporter, told me at the time. "You can't support or ignore what this administration is doing and say you're pro-women's rights."

An employee of one of the organizations involved in the rally told me that leadership at their organization "explicitly said we can't speak" on Israel and Palestine. "They're always touting things like, 'Believe Black women,' 'trust women of color,' but when it actually comes to practicing their values, they don't," the employee said. Citing their experience working in fundraising, the employee said they suspect national women's organizations are "choosing to fall in line with oppressive systems because it benefits them," pointing to how aligning with Democratic politicians is often required for fundraising. "These organizations will do anything to not affect their donor base."

Bracey Sherman told me she'd been invited to the *Roe* anniversary rally by the Biden-Harris campaign but declined over its treatment of Palestinian women as well as the administration's lack of material advocacy for abortion access. To her, that some women's groups could continue to unconditionally, publicly support Biden for merely identifying as "pro-choice," while other feminists protest his treatment of Palestinian women, elucidated the difference between reproductive rights and reproductive justice—the latter of which is a framework that challenges different systems of oppression and white supremacy, and demands exponentially more than the restoration of *Roe* alone.

Reproductive justice organizations like Indigenous Women Rising, the National Network of Abortion Funds, and the Feminist Women's Health Center signed a letter identifying Palestinian liberation as a core part of their movement early on amid Israel's escalating attacks on Gaza in October 2023. "Zionism is a contradiction to Reproductive Justice," the letter states. "At its core, Zionism denies Palestinians the right to exist, thrive, and have autonomy over their bodies, something that impacts Palestinians of all genders and ages."[6] In December 2023, hundreds of Planned Parenthood rank-and-file employees wrote a letter criticizing their organization for its insufficient response to the crisis in Gaza—and particularly the organization's silence after a health center of an International Planned Parenthood Federation affiliate was destroyed by Israeli forces months earlier.[7]

"Reproductive freedom doesn't stop at our borders," Bracey Sherman told me. "It is not liberation for me as a Black woman to have abortion access on the backs of dead Palestinians."

Despite Biden's relative inability to point to meaningful policy achievements on abortion, his campaign made significant demands of pro-choice voters—for money, for a Democratic Congress, for unconditional support—all, of course, while using our tax dollars to fund genocide and reproductive violence abroad. At the core of these contradictions is the tension between the neoliberal movement for reproductive rights, a movement centering federal electoral politics and frequent, crushing compromises, and the transformative movement for reproductive justice. The Biden campaign reflected the futility and outright violence of the federal electoral gambit for reproductive rights, at a core moment in history. But even prior to *Dobbs*, for years, Democratic politicians in Congress and the

White House fundraised off the perpetual threat to abortion rights, arguably enabling this threat through each election cycle to be able to do so.

Democrats held almost total power on the federal level in the early years of the Obama era to codify a right to abortion. But President Obama stated outright that abortion rights were "not a priority" for his administration in 2009.[8] Even after 2009, Democrats have theoretically had the power to abolish the filibuster—a Senate rule that requires a more decisive majority to pass legislation—to pass a right to abortion. As journalist Danielle Tcholakian pointed out in an essay in the spring of 2022, "They've refused to, because it was more politically expedient to win votes by fear. Vote for Democrats so *Roe* doesn't get overturned was their preferred way, always the Democratic way."

"Why achieve new things, why take risks, why try, when you could just scare people away from a potential brighter future with the fear of a darker one?" Tcholakian wrote. "We won't do anything, but the other side will and it'll be bad, so please click this donation button and turn out to vote." This is fundamentally coercive and, as the outcome of the 2024 election proved, ineffective.

Within moments of *Dobbs*, fundraising emails from Democratic leadership began pouring in, and they haven't stopped. But despite this fundraising, Democratic elected officials offered few promises and little of anything where the restoration of our rights was concerned. Texas Rep. Henry Cuellar—a proud anti-abortion Democrat who won reelection that year with support from then-Speaker Nancy Pelosi and party leadership— simply reiterated that he was "pro-life." Biden, too, reiterated his stance against abolishing the filibuster or expanding the Supreme Court—basically, doing anything that might be vaguely helpful.

The consequences of liberal politicians' failures on reproductive rights cut beyond the U.S. citizenry alone: Amid news that the Supreme Court intended to overturn *Roe*, Oklahoma Gov. Kevin Stitt declared his intent to violate Indigenous sovereignty and find a path to ban abortion on tribal land, too. Oklahoma has the second largest population of Native American people in the country. "Oklahomans will not think very well of that [abortion services on tribal land] if tribes try to set up abortion clinics," Stitt said in 2022. "They think that you can be 1/1,000th tribal member and not have to follow the state law."

Liberal reproductive rights advocates took immediate issue with this—in some cases because this would theoretically block the ability of non-Native people to travel to tribal land to seek abortion care for themselves. At the time, Indigenous Women Rising's Rachael Lorenzo expressed her frustration to me with both Stitt's stated desire to violate Indigenous sovereignty, and self-serving liberal voices. Abortion among Indigenous communities long predates American empire, they (Lorenzo uses they-them pronouns) told me: "We were already raising our families the best ways we knew how, and we knew based on the circumstances we were in—through famine, drought, whether it was time for migration—when it was not time to expand our family," they said. "It was just since 1492 since Columbus and his dumb ass arrived at this part of the world, that was the beginning of the removal of our bodily autonomy." As for the idea that it would be in the interests of "pro-choice," liberal, non-Indigenous activists to advocate for abortion rights on tribal land for their own benefit: "Our lands are not just places to skirt laws," Lorenzo said.

They also noted the inevitable risks to Native American communities that go hand in hand with increased presence of non-Indigenous people on tribal land: "One of the factors that contributes to the many missing and murdered Indigenous women and girls is that many of our abusers and predators are non-Native people, who know and take advantage of how tribes often don't have the legal standing to charge them or to prosecute them."

The path forward for justice for pregnant people and survivors requires us to reject the ineptitude and fecklessness of neoliberal politicians and their self-serving electoral goals. Immediately after *Roe*, the Democratic rank-and-file accepted the Hyde Amendment in 1976, a policy to prohibit federal funding for most abortions that remains attached to the federal budget to this day; they accepted a slew of state-level abortion restrictions throughout the 2010s; they've turned a blind eye to abortion and pregnancy criminalization for decades. In the 1990s, the stigmatizing "safe, legal, and rare" slogan emerged as the party's go-to talking point, meant to distinguish acceptable abortions from frivolous ones. Concession after concession from "pro-choice," federal politicians is why we're here today.

Shortly after *Dobbs*, Democrats leaned in heavily on the promise to "restore *Roe*" and stop Republican anti-abortion extremism—all while unequivocally supporting Israel in its genocidal war on Gaza. Many of these Democrats received substantial funding from prominent pro-Israel lobbyist groups, which simultaneously funded anti-abortion lawmakers. The American Israel Public Affairs Committee (AIPAC) alone endorsed and funded over 200 anti-abortion Republicans in the 2024 election cycle—including dozens who voted for or even co-authored extreme, anti-abortion legislation like the Life at Conception Act, which would establish fetal personhood. AIPAC also waged an almost unprecedentedly aggressive spending campaign to unseat Democratic Congress members like Cori Bush and Jamaal Bowman, who advocated early on for a ceasefire in Gaza. Bush has spoken openly about her abortion experience after surviving sexual assault, and was a leader on these issues. According to a Politico report from June 2024, about half of donors who gave to Democratic candidates via AIPAC for the 2024 cycle had also given to anti-abortion Republican candidates since 2020.[9] The Zionist and anti-abortion movements are fundamentally far-right ideologies.

By design, within a political system driven by the rat race for reelection, by lobbyist interests, by apathy to the lives and struggles of pregnant people from the U.S. to Palestine, this is our reality: one in which *Roe* is held over our heads, while our calls for an end to genocide and violent colonial occupation are ignored. Federal electoralism has always failed on reproductive and survivor justice, and it's paramount that we direct our care and effort elsewhere to meaningfully fight for pregnant people and survivors.

Conclusion

Beyond *Roe*

The end of *Roe* and ensuing era of abortion bans is unsurvivable without community, without friends and loved ones and often enough strangers willing to pool together resources, offer an out-of-state abortion seeker a spare bed to sleep on, and refuse to turn each other in to law enforcement or other authorities.

In October 2024, Marcus Silva and Jonathan Mitchell dropped their lawsuit against the women who had helped Silva's wife have an abortion two years earlier. At the end of Silva's lawsuit, two of the women, Jackie Noyola and Amy Carpenter, told me they hoped their case wouldn't dissuade anyone from helping others—that, after all, is the point of legal harassment campaigns. Noyola said:

> While we are grateful this fraudulent case is finally over, we are angry for ourselves and others who have been terrorized for the simple act of supporting a friend who is facing abuse. No one should ever have to fear punishment, criminalization, or a lengthy court battle for helping someone they care about.

Her hope is that despite Mitchell and Silva's attempt to make an example of her, Carpenter, and their friend, people "will still want to keep helping each other and not be afraid."

The federal right to abortion is gone. It's a harrowing reality that's since borne horrific consequences. But it's also a time of reckoning and truth—including the truth that presidential elections and ceaseless political games will never protect our dignity and bodily autonomy from the institutions set out to harm us as designed.

As lawmakers and elected officials continue to hold hostage our most fundamental human rights to abortion, mutual aid has long kept pregnant people and survivors afloat. Abolitionist scholar-activist Ruth Wilson Gilmore has often said that abolition—the dismantling of carceral systems of violence, such as the punishing prison industrial complex and the intertwining social and economic systems that drive it—is a physical place: Abolition is a set of material conditions, the reconstruction of society to care for rather than punish, isolate, and kill us, not platitudes and niceties from ultra-rich politicians. "'Freedom is a place' means we combine resources, ingenuity, and commitment to produce the conditions in which life is precious for all," Gilmore told me in a conversation in 2022 about her book *Abolition Geography*. Across the country, mutual aid networks redistribute wealth, bridge gaps, and fund logistical arrangements for people to afford abortion and contraception, as well as transportation, lodging, and child care to travel across state lines and reach these resources, or legal funds for those who face punishment. Some funds, like Kentucky Health Justice Network, also devote vital resources to trans people who face added barriers to reach abortion and other sexual and reproductive health care as well as gender-affirming care. Texas' Jane's Due Process organization provides legal support and other resources for minors and young people in the state who face added restrictions to get reproductive care. The Mariposa Fund specializes in serving undocumented abortion seekers, who face substantially greater risks in crossing state lines to get care due to checkpoints scattered across Texas. Indigenous Women Rising funds abortion and reproductive care for Indigenous and young people.

Our post-*Roe* times require us to lift the work of abortion funds; understand how to protect ourselves, pregnant people, and survivors from the criminal legal system and its extensive surveillance apparatuses; and support mutual aid-based networks of support for survivors. They require us to care and look out for not just ourselves but each other.

When it comes to pregnancy and safety from state surveillance and criminalization, Cynthia Conti-Cook, the author of "Surveilling the Digital Abortion Diary" whose insight I also included earlier in this book, told me in 2022 that we've largely been left to fend for ourselves. This is possible, she said, with use of encrypted messaging apps like Signal, encrypted email like Proton Mail, and virtual private networks, or VPNs. "When we're thinking about what digital routines we're willing to incorporate in our own lives for our safety, we should think about not just how this issue impacts us, but how it impacts the person in our networks who's most vulnerable," she explained. "When you're thinking, 'Do I go through the trouble of getting on Signal or Wire?'—we should be thinking about the person who might be most vulnerable to prosecution, or some [Texas S.B. 8] litigation."

Educating ourselves about our rights, our privacy, and the resources available to us when in need of abortion and other forms of reproductive care, or experiencing domestic violence, or in need of medical help but afraid of being reported to police, isn't just an act of self-preservation. It's an act of being in community. It's an act of preparing ourselves to help loved ones or strangers who may need us in the future. At all times, consider and take action to protect the safety of abuse victims, people of color, low-income people, queer and trans people, and those who are already over-policed by law enforcement and marginalized within the medical and criminal legal systems. Store and share the contact information of pregnancy-related legal defense resources like If/When/How's Repro Legal Defense Fund or Pregnancy Justice, as well as the M+A Hotline (a 24/7 hotline for anonymous medical advice from pro-abortion rights doctors). Keep medication abortion on hand in advance, for yourself or anyone you care about who may need it in the future; groups like Plan C Pills, Aid Access, and Hey Jane are always standing by to help individuals access these medications, at discounted prices or even for free. Connect domestic violence survivors with the National Domestic Violence Hotline, or victims who may be struggling with unwanted, unsafe pregnancies to the National Network of Abortion Funds. In a capitalist economic system where need is endless and yet the resources available to us are sparse, be mindful of how we prioritize donations—to direct services, mutual aid, and legal defense funds, for example, always before political campaigns. Strategic participation in electoral politics, specifically at the most local levels, can produce sometimes life-saving outcomes. City councils in Austin, Texas, and New York, New York, for example, have voted to allocate city funds to support abortion access, and state lawmakers have led the charge to enshrine abortion rights into state constitutions sans *Roe*. But it's also vitally important to question how the same, often performatively pro-abortion rights "allies" in federal office who did virtually nothing to prevent or urgently respond to *Dobbs* so often preach to us that voting for them is the only solution. They are the beneficiaries of a dehumanizing and transactional political system that positions our rights and survival as a fundraising ploy for powerful elites.

In 2023, Nebraska Democrats narrowly defeated a six-week abortion ban after extensive, contentious debate among even anti-abortion lawmakers about whether its exceptions would sufficiently protect doctors who provide emergency care. The proposed ban fell one vote short of getting the votes needed to overcome the Democrats' filibuster. State Sen. Megan Hunt, an Independent who's been vocally critical of the Democratic party's lack of meaningful investments in pro-abortion rights state and local lawmakers in states like Nebraska, was instrumental to stopping the bill. "We decided early in the session, this first one after *Roe*, that every bill was an abortion bill," Hunt told me that spring. "That means, we were going to fight on every single bill, use any influence we could get, to be able to change the ultimate vote on an abortion ban like this." She and her pro-abortion rights colleagues filibustered, stalled, and otherwise increased pressure to remind Republicans that the consequence of supporting an abortion ban would be total stagnation in the legislature. "It's to the point that typically, we pass maybe 300 or 400 bills per session. In this session, we're on track to pass 20, 25, because we're filibustering every single bill."

Hunt emphasized that she and her colleagues achieved this win with little national attention and "without a penny of support" from national Democratic leadership and top Democratic PACs: "We're out here scrapping, fighting, winning, and it should be a lesson to everybody that you don't need to be noticed to do the right thing. You don't need to have financial backing, you don't need to be on CNN or what-the-fuck-ever. In Nebraska, we're fighting and winning."

For years now, culminating in the first presidential election after *Dobbs*, there hasn't been a credible opposition party to anti-abortion Republicans on the federal level. So, abortion funds, legal advocacy groups, and domestic violence shelters and mutual aid networks have taken on the monumental task—and it's their work that deserves our support, financial contributions, and dedication, rather than Democratic party elites.

Ballot Box Realities

In 2024, organizers in ten states successfully collected enough signatures to place abortion rights proposals on their ballots. They managed this, even as collecting the hundreds of thousands of signatures necessary was far more complicated than it should have been. In every state where abortion rights activists were working to get a ballot measure approved, anti-abortion activists perpetrated shameless harassment, intimidation campaigns, and outright lies to try to stop their efforts. Deception has become the standard from the anti-abortion movement, Kelly Hall, executive director of Fairness Project, told me, because "they know or fear they're going to lose a conversation about the substance of the issue."

The groundswell of support for abortion rights—even in deep red states and swing states—was unsurprising to Hall, whose organization has been fundraising and organizing for abortion rights ballot measures across the country including in Arizona and Ohio since *Dobbs*. "A lot of our political coverage is presented through this partisan lens with voters thinking of themselves as 'red' or 'blue,' but people support a lot of different issues across the spectrum regardless of political identity," Hall said. "We're seeing overwhelming support for abortion rights, record-shattering numbers of people saying 'we want to vote on this issue ourselves and this shouldn't be political football.'" (Importantly, of course, abortion rights supporters should probably consider that electing an anti-abortion president or anti-abortion government officials could severely undermine any progress achieved through a successful abortion rights ballot measure.)

Seven out of ten states successfully passed their abortion rights ballot measures; Missouri became the first state in the nation to pass a measure to repeal a currently active, total abortion ban. Floridians decisively voted for abortion rights, too, as their measure received 57% of the vote, but the state's anti-democratic 60% threshold for ballot measures tanked it.

Anti-democratic policies reign when it comes to enshrining abortion rights on the state level. Throughout the campaign trail in 2024, Donald Trump maintained that he would let individual states decide on abortion rights—given his record of anti-abortion extremism, this was pure obfuscation. And it was also irrelevant. Only 19 states allow voters rather than the legislature to directly put measures on the ballot. Many states that don't offer a direct citizen initiative process also enforce total bans, like Texas, Georgia, Alabama, and Tennessee. And in the states that do allow voters to put measures on the ballot, the built-in challenges can be insurmountable. There's Florida's 60% threshold for ballot measures, or Colorado's 55% threshold, or disinformation campaigns and legal attacks and obstruction from anti-abortion government officials. These are acts of desperation because abortion rights are popular.

It's a mistake to divide states by red or blue, by which can or can't be saved, at the expense of pregnant people, survivors, and marginalized communities who don't have the liberty of leaving and fleeing their states' violent abortion laws. Not only can some people not move away from abortion-banned states, but some are forced to move to or live in these states by their employers. This is the case for some members of the military. And, in January 2025, Meta CEO Mark Zuckerberg issued a requirement for safety and content moderators at his company to move from California to Texas, ostensibly to eliminate "political bias." Of course, being forced by your employer to move to a state with an abortion ban that's killed at least three people is about as "politically biased" as it gets. Meta has also faced criticism from abortion rights activists for years for censoring medically accurate information and resources to access abortion.

Aimee Arrambide, executive director of the abortion rights group Avow Texas, has been organizing for reproductive rights in the state for decades. "It's so insulting to the people that have been on the ground doing this work for decades, trying to ensure access to no avail, to act like you have the answers and we don't," she said in 2022. "And the answer absolutely isn't to only have a few sanctuary states, and then half the country has to travel far distances, spend lots and lots of money, in order to access basic medical care that we should have within our own community."

Abortion bans in red states can't just be fundraising pitches for liberal politicians in solidly blue states, or fodder for viral posts from New York City-based liberal activists. To Indigenous Women Rising's Rachael Lorenzo, there was always something achingly familiar about the notion that people subjected to the abortion laws in their states—or countries—should just leave. It's a gentler, more insidious way of pushing people off their land, out of their homes—and it's rooted in colonial conceptions of gender and bodies. Through her work leading Avow, Arrambide told me she's all too familiar with uphill battles in her state, and thrilled by abortion-related legislative victories in other states. Laws like these, rather than fundraising pitches from liberal, blue-state politicians, are what create change, and it's on all of us to educate ourselves, each other, and advocate for abortion access within our own communities. Progress toward reproductive justice in any community, in any state, empowers people everywhere.

Around the World and Back

In recent years, the tide of reproductive rights has risen and fallen all around the world, sometimes in opposition. It was only in 2018 that Ireland federally legalized abortion, overturning a national ban that had forced many people to travel out-of-country for vital health care, or sometimes die from pregnancy-related complications—a gruesome phenomenon that's increasingly playing out in the U.S. and across Latin America. Several countries have recently taken steps to loosen abortion bans while others have, by contrast, moved to further crack down on abortion access. In 2021, Mexico's Supreme Court ruled that abortion can't be treated as a crime in the northern border state of Coahuila, and in the fall of 2023, the court decriminalized abortion across the country. But at the same time, since *Dobbs*, lawmakers in the Dominican Republic and Brazil have taken a page from the playbook of the U.S. anti-abortion movement to further restrict the health service. In the Dominican Republic, in the summer of 2024, the Senate passed a law doubling down on the country's total, exception-free abortion ban—the same law also "reduces penalties for sexual violence within marriage, classified as 'non-consensual sexual activity,' and continues to exclude sexual orientation from the list of characteristics protected from discrimination," Human Rights Watch reported at the time.[1] The Dominican Republic is one of five countries in Latin America and the Caribbean that maintain total, criminal abortion bans for both abortion patients and providers.

In Brazil, where abortion is banned except to save the lives of rape victims or in rare cases of fetal anencephaly, journalist Garnet Henderson reported in 2024 that anti-abortion crisis pregnancy centers—like those in the U.S.—were beginning to emerge across the country to deceive and entrap pregnant people. The influence of violent anti-abortion forces in the U.S. can't be understated: CPCs are an invention of the U.S. anti-abortion movement, and these propaganda machines are spreading around the world. In Brazil, all of this is unfolding as sexual violence rates in the country are at an all-time high.[2] Elsewhere in Latin America, in 2015, a ten-year-old Paraguayan rape victim was forced to carry a pregnancy to term after officials denied her mother's plea for an abortion, drawing global attention and outrage. The child lived, but three years later, a 14-year-old Paraguayan girl, also impregnated by rape, died in childbirth after also being denied an abortion by the government.

In 2021, Argentina legalized abortion up to 14 weeks into a pregnancy. But years before that, in 2014, a woman named Belén (a pseudonym) went to a local hospital serving low-income communities in Tucuman, Argentina, experiencing severe abdominal pain; days later, she left in handcuffs after experiencing a miscarriage while not even knowing she was pregnant. She was jailed for two years. In the 2024 book *What Happened to Belén? The Unjust Imprisonment That Sparked a Women's Rights Movement* by Ana Elena Correa, Belén recounted that, as she lay in severe pain in her hospital bed, a nurse made her look at her fetal remains and told her, "This is your son. Look what you did, bitch." Still reeling from her miscarriage, Belén was separated from her family and taken to a jail across the street from the hospital, symbolizing the inextricability of the medical and criminal systems. Her family sought criminal defense lawyers who charged them exorbitant fees, only to actively sabotage Belén because they believed she was guilty. In *What Happened to Belén?*, Correa tells the story of the women attorneys who took Belén's case and won her freedom through both legal advocacy and organizing a mass, global movement for cultural change;

eventually, her story paved the way for a successful, global public pressure campaign to legalize abortion.

"The doctors who accused me are still living their lives," Belén wrote while in jail. "The men who convicted me get to go on like nothing happened . . . They don't know what it's like waking up in the same place every day, being away from your family every day." She continued, "They tortured me . . . They sentenced me and then they washed their hands. Now I want them to fix it."

The recent trajectory of Poland's anti-abortion state violence, meanwhile, presents an increasingly unsettling glimpse at a future that the U.S. seems to be barreling toward. In 2022, a year after a total abortion ban took effect in the country, a second woman died after being forced to carry a dead fetus for a whole week, denied life-saving abortion care for a nonviable pregnancy.[3] Months later, the Polish government announced it was rolling out a plan to establish a nationalized, government-run registry of pregnancies, ensuring all miscarriages and pregnancy outcomes would innately become objects of state suspicion and surveillance.[4] In 2023, Polish police were so desperate to investigate and potentially prosecute a woman for an alleged abortion that they searched sewage for her terminated fetal remains.[5] Later that year, reports emerged that the Polish government successfully developed tests that can detect remains of abortion pills, where, previously, if taken orally the pills were untraceable, rendering medication abortions indistinguishable from miscarriages.[6]

Around the same time the Polish government began developing these tests, activist Justyna Wydrzyńska began serving an eight-month prison sentence for shipping medication abortion to a domestic violence victim trying to flee her abusive relationship back in 2020. At the start of Wydrzyńska's trial, she told the *Guardian* in 2022 she'd been contacted by a woman who was twelve weeks pregnant and experiencing domestic violence at the height of the COVID pandemic. "I had my abortion at 12 weeks and I have also been in an abusive relationship," Wydrzyńska said. "I know what it means to be in this situation. Helping her was my first human response."[7]

The woman who contacted Wydrzyńska had previously tried to travel to Germany to get an abortion, but had been stopped by her husband. Wydrzyńska said she realized they were "running out of time" and directly sent the woman abortion pills that Wydrzyńska had kept in her home. When the package arrived, the woman's husband called the police, ultimately leading her to miscarry out of distress. Over a year later, police came to Wydrzyńska's home, confiscated her remaining abortion pills and the computers of her and her children, and charged her with illegally aiding an abortion. She told the *Guardian* that, for her 15 years as an abortion rights activist, the Polish government wanted to use her case "to make an example out of me and send me to jail, maybe even for years."

The door is wide open for Poland's reality to become reality in the United States—or in any country. The descent to fascism, paired with patriarchal state violence against pregnant people and survivors, is a global phenomenon; the fates of systematically oppressed communities around the world are intertwined. In 2024, citing the *Dobbs* decision, Uganda's Constitutional Court issued a ruling that upheld most of the provisions of a law that imposes the death penalty—by hanging—on people convicted of "aggravated homosexuality": "In [*Dobbs*], the U.S. Supreme Court considered the nation's history and traditions, as well as the dictates of democracy and rule of law, to overrule the broader right to autonomy," the Ugandan court determined.

The court considered the implications of upholding the right to autonomy under the guise of personal dignity . . . and held that it was time to return the permissibility of abortion and the limitations thereon to the people's elected representatives as demanded by the Constitution and the rule of law. This is precisely what was done with the issue of homosexuality in Uganda.

The implications of *Dobbs*—for pregnant people, for abuse victims, for those marginalized by the health system, for communities of color, for LGBTQ people—are global. We owe it to the global community to resist and meaningfully challenge this state violence, because our plights are deeply and fundamentally connected.

Toward Reproductive Justice

After activist Alison Turkos survived being kidnapped and gang-raped on a Lyft ride in New York in 2017, when we spoke a few years later, she told me her commitment to reproductive justice only deepened from that experience. "Survivors and someone who's seeking abortion care want the same thing—we want control over our bodies, at any time, for any reason," she said. Her words have stayed with me. As a survivor, myself, I've often reflected on how a rape doesn't end with a rape; it's followed by everything the world does to you after. Abusers and the state often collude to enforce an endless feedback loop of violence against rape victims, against pregnant people, against those who are left without options.

Survivor and reproductive justice are intertwined, both existential fights against pervading, patriarchal state violence. "Abortion is the most critical way to protect victims, help them out of an unsafe situation, not prolong their connection to someone who's assaulted them," Prairie Fund's Destini Spaeth told me. At this increasingly dire moment, what's happened before and what's happening now paint an urgent picture of the way forward—this requires us to understand the anti-abortion movement's endgame of "fetal personhood" to violently render pregnant people as subhuman; reject the political games of neoliberal politicians, who insist on our votes to "save *Roe*" while facilitating reproductive violence abroad; and center and protect survivors and pregnant people through models of community-based care.

In Supreme Court Justice Samuel Alito's opinion overturning *Roe* in 2022, he wrote that "abortion is not deeply rooted in the Nation's history and tradition." This is a lie. Explicit abortion bans and criminalization, We Testify's Renee Bracey Sherman told me, are a far, far newer invention in this country than abortion. "Everyone was having abortions freely until the institutions of colonialism, capitalism, policing—all rooted in white supremacy, all one and the same," she said, as we spoke about *Liberating Abortion*, the book she co-authored with journalist Regina Mahone, in 2024. While liberal activists and politicians today center their demands around restoring *Roe*—a precedent that left large swaths of the U.S. without convenient and affordable abortion access—historically, abortions in varying forms were once a day-to-day fact of life without government interference. On several occasions during his presidency, President Biden insisted he doesn't like abortion and doesn't support "abortion on demand." But generations ago, Bracey Sherman said, civil rights activists and feminists had no trouble articulating that what they wanted—and were absolutely correct to want—was, indeed, *abortion on demand*.

CONCLUSION: BEYOND *ROE*

We are increasingly in uncharted territory. But our histories and our communities can always guide us.

The current landscape around abortion is bleak. And bleaker, still, is that in the face of something of a blank slate, an opportunity to establish a new framework for bodily autonomy and reproductive justice, liberal political leaders are fighting for crumbs. So, the work falls on us, as it always has. When we expand our imagination beyond the limits of a government system that has never honored our humanity, when we set our sights on the people around us, on our communities and all the things big and small that we can most directly impact, we start building toward reproductive justice. And we can do that with or without *Roe*.

Afterword

In February 2025, Harold Thompson of Texas was sentenced to life in prison for the 2023 murder of his partner, Gabriela Gonzalez, for having an abortion. As I took in the news, I hoped it would bring her family some measure of peace. But I also thought of other women and pregnant people who have been killed, or pushed to the brink of death, or subjected to long-term health consequences from abortion bans. Their killer, their abuser, is the state. And under Donald Trump's second presidency, their suffering has already worsened—in the U.S. and around the world.

Within days of Pam Bondi's confirmation as Trump's attorney general in February 2025, she met with Louisiana's governor, attorney general, and law enforcement officials who sought her help creating "consistency" in federal policy around mailing abortion pills across state lines. They also sought Bondi's support in their criminal case against a New York doctor who allegedly mailed the pills to a Louisiana mother and daughter; in front of reporters, Bondi said she "would love to help" them. Shortly after that meeting, Louisiana officials signed an extradition warrant for the doctor, Margaret Carpenter. "Dr. Carpenter needs to be careful with her travel plans," Louisiana's attorney general said on social media. "If New York won't cooperate, there are other states that will." Attorney Alejandra Caraballo, co-author of the 2023 CUNY law review article *Extradition in Post-Roe America*, told me the state's quest to extradite Carpenter—alongside Texas' civil lawsuit against Carpenter, filed in December 2024—could reach the Supreme Court. Contentious interstate extradition cases are rare, complicated by the fact that Carpenter isn't a "fugitive," because she didn't commit a crime in Louisiana and flee. "We haven't really seen this kind of disparity in state laws around human rights since the Civil War, where, what constitutes a human right in one state, constitutes a capital crime in another," Caraballo said. "The federal Constitution is not set up to manage that. The last time we had this kind of disparity led to the full breakdown of calamity of the states, to the Civil War."

As a result of Louisiana's pursuit of Carpenter, she was trapped in the state of New York. "I think there's a reason we're seeing [anti-abortion] states take these actions now and not a year ago," Caraballo said. The Trump-run Justice Department could bring federal charges against Carpenter or other doctors like her under the Comstock Act. And it's not impossible that Trump "will simply send federal marshals and bypass the extradition process," Caraballo said.

Within the first weeks of Trump's presidency, he took swift, devastating action on reproductive health. He immediately reinstated the global gag rule, which bars organizations that receive U.S. funding from performing or educating about abortion, impeding their ability to provide a range of services including contraception, HIV treatment, child nutrition, water sanitation, malaria, and tuberculosis; when Trump enacted the gag rule in his first term, International Planned Parenthood Federation warned the cuts would yield "3.3 million more abortions, most of which will be forced to occur in unsafe settings, 15,000 more maternal deaths, and 8 million more unintended pregnancies." At the same time, Trump issued pardons to about two dozen U.S. anti-abortion activists who were convicted for not only illegally barricading abortion clinics, but in some cases, violently attacking patients and clinic staff. At the same time, his Justice Department announced it would severely limit enforcement of the FACE Act, allowing anti-abortion protesters to obstruct, harass, or assault abortion clinics, patients, and staff with impunity—barring "extraordinary circumstances." As Slate put it, Trump effectively declared "open season" on abortion providers.

Similarly terrifying developments swept the nation on the state-level within weeks of Trump's presidency, with top anti-abortion activists and groups proclaiming his reelection a mandate for further extremism—like Texas Right to Life's recruitment campaign seeking abusive men to sue partners who have abortions. The Texas attorney general's office is reportedly facilitating a similar recruitment operation, per the *Washington Post* in January 2025, which is how the state found a man who reported his partner's abortion with pills sent from Carpenter in New York, triggering the state's suit against her. A Texas judge ruled in February 2025 that Carpenter owed Texas over $100,000 in damages. This is part of anti-abortion states' broader effort to entrap their residents and expand the parameters of their bans, in a direct challenge to pro-abortion states' shield laws. It's also part of a cruel, broader effort to expand the carceral apparatus: While New York state is protecting Carpenter, the Louisiana mother to whom Carpenter mailed the pills faces criminal charges and the threat of jail.

Without evidence, Louisiana officials say the mother coerced her underage daughter to take the pills. Anti-abortion officials are increasingly pushing the lie that abortion access feeds domestic abuse, claiming abusive partners or family members are "coercing" vulnerable people like domestic violence victims or children to have abortions. Louisiana in 2024 became the first state to criminalize possession of abortion pills for most people; the law's authors justified it by citing the tragic case of a man who fed his partner abortion pills without her consent. A handful of states, including Texas, Indiana, Idaho, and Kentucky, immediately introduced legislation to similarly criminalize prescribing or possessing medication for abortion in January 2025. Abortion pills have been indispensable for people in all states to continue to access abortion under bans; now, that's all under threat, purportedly to help abuse victims while, in reality, entrapping them. Ironically, anti-abortion activists are openly seeking and collaborating with none other than abusive men to trigger lawsuits and try to ban mailing abortion pills altogether.

Every new piece of data that comes to light post-*Dobbs* further elucidates the violence and brutality of abortion bans, particularly for the most vulnerable, including survivors and child abuse victims. In January 2025, the Texas Health Department published data that showed in 2023, at least 105 minors had to leave the state for abortion care; at least six were children under twelve years old. That number—105—is ninefold what it was five years earlier. Prior to *Dobbs*, between 1,000 and 1,400 Texas minors received abortions in the state annually; that number fell to zero in 2023. Child welfare advocates told the *Houston Chronicle* many of the minors' pregnancies resulted from rape. Around the same time, a study published in *JAMA* revealed a sharp rise in infant mortality rates in states that have banned abortion. *ProPublica* simultaneously reported that since Texas' 2021 ban, the sepsis rate among people who were hospitalized while losing a pregnancy in the second trimester surged by more than 50%.

Sepsis is a leading cause of death in hospitals across the U.S., and people with nonviable pregnancies face higher risk of sepsis the longer fetal tissue remains in their uterus; the state's maternal mortality rate skyrocketed in kind.

As always, anti-abortion leaders remain unmoved by the consequences of their laws; they see abortion seekers as deserving of what fate befalls them under abortion bans, and they see child rape victims, or people who experience horrific complications, as a fair price to pay for total, state control over our bodies and lives. Also in January 2025, four states—South Carolina, North Dakota, Indiana, and Oklahoma—introduced bills to reclassify abortion as homicide; in three of those states, abortion patients could potentially qualify for the death penalty for homicide. "The more of these kinds of bills that get introduced, people get numb to the idea of them, and they seem less and less radical," Pregnancy Justice's Dana Sussman told the *Guardian* at the time. Whether bills like this pass or take multiple tries, the Overton window is clearly shifting, priming us to eventually accept what might seem unthinkable right now.

At the same time as those bills, Missouri Republicans introduced a bill to establish a state-run registry of potential abortion seekers as well as a state-run adoption marketplace, which one advocate compared to "eHarmony for babies." Both would be run by "contractors"—presumably anti-abortion crisis pregnancy centers, which have been surveilling and ensnaring abortion seekers for years, with millions in state funding. Montana, meanwhile, introduced a bill to criminalize traveling abortion seekers, charging them with "trafficking" their fetuses. And West Virginia Republicans repeatedly introduced legislation to end their abortion ban's narrow rape exception, effectively declaring "unborn children" more worthy of protection than born, living child rape victims.

It would feel dishonest to look someone in the eye right now and tell them, without condition, that everything will be fine. But hope is a muscle, and all around us, there are still reasons to flex it. The right to abortion is more popular than ever; the overwhelming majority of survey respondents in 2024 told Axios the government shouldn't intervene in pregnancy decisions, period. There's a reason Trump and anti-abortion candidates broadly went to such lengths to avoid speaking about abortion ahead of the first presidential election post-*Dobbs*.

For decades, the anti-abortion movement wielded subtlety as its weapon of choice; lawmakers devastated abortion access across the country via insidious restrictions, many predicated on faux concerns for "women's safety," all while driving up maternal mortality rates and isolating abuse victims from life-saving services. But *Roe* stood, so a feeling of safety and consequent passivity pervaded.

Those days are over.

As the current, global tide of fascism surges, as far-right politicians consolidate power at every level, and the supposed "opposition" party largely cowers with its tail between its legs, complacency among everyday people is no longer an option. We are at a critical point, a crossroads for not just our bodily autonomy, but any amount of personal and political self-determination, safeguards from state violence, the containment of American imperialism at its most vile. A second Trump presidency will not offer respite for any of what I've detailed in this book. Rather than running from that grave reality, we should stand up to it.

The truth in all its brutality is often radicalizing: If state violence and cruelty are the only answer our top elected officials and institutions have ever been able to come up with, it's past time for those of us who are sick of that answer to turn to our communities, and each other, for different ones.

February 2025

Notes

Introduction

1. Erik Eckholm, "Custody Battle Raises Questions About the Rights of Women," *New York Times*, (November 2013). www.nytimes. com/2013/11/24/us/custody-battle-raises-questions-about-the-rights-of-women.html (last accessed May 2024).
2. "Respite in Miller Custody Case," Associated Press, (December 2013). www.nytimes.com/2013/12/10/sports/skiing/respite-in-miller-custody-case.html (last accessed May 2024).
3. *New York Times*, (November 2013).
4. https://americanpregnancy.org/healthy-pregnancy/general/pregnancy-and-divorce/ (last accessed May 2024).
5. www.pregnancyjusticeus.org/wp-content/uploads/2022/12/fetal-personhood-with-appendix-UPDATED-1.pdf (last accessed May 2024).
6. Centers for Disease Control and Prevention, www.cdc.gov/maternal-mortality/php/data-research/mmrc-2017-2019.html (last accessed May 2024).
7. Maeve E. Wallace, Charles Stoecker, Sydney Sauter, and Dovile Vilda, Health Affairs, (May 2024). www.healthaffairs.org/doi/abs/10.1377/hlthaff.2023.01098?journalCode=hlthaff
8. https://pubmed.ncbi.nlm.nih.gov/8754670/ (last accessed May 2024).
9. https://jamanetwork.com/journals/jamapsychiatry/fullarticle/10.1001/jamapsychiatry.2022.4394?guestAccessKey=9ac07a88-f8d6-40c4-b074-8b1a0311fafo&utm_source=For_The_Media&utm_medium=referral&utm_campaign=ftm_links&utm_content=tfl&utm_term=122822 (last accessed May 2024).
10. www.jezebel.com/domestic-violence-hotline-reports-99-increase-in-calls-1850641660 (last accessed May 2024).

11. www.jezebel.com/domestic-violence-hotline-reports-99-increase-in-calls-1850641660 (last accessed May 2024).

12. www.jezebel.com/post-dobbs-abortion-bans-have-given-abusers-a-new-power (last accessed May 2024).

13. www.washingtonpost.com/politics/2024/11/20/antiabortion-crack-down-pills/ (last accessed November 2024).

14. www.tpr.org/public-health/2024-11-25/domestic-violence-shelters-in-texas-see-a-surge-of-pregnant-women-after-the-dobbs-decision (last accessed December 2024).

15. www.propublica.org/article/texas-abortion-ban-exceptions-deaths (last accessed November 2024).

16. https://jezebel.com/rape-induced-pregnancy-roe-dobbs-abortion-ban-1851209068 (last accessed May 2024).

17. Jessica Valenti, *Abortion* (New York: Penguin Random House, 2024). (last accessed October 2024).

18. www.ansirh.org/research/ongoing/turnaway-study (last accessed May 2024).

19. https://jezebel.com/sexual-assault-survivors-are-being-billed-thousands-for-1849534311 (last accessed May 2024).

20. https://idahocapitalsun.com/2024/04/05/idaho-is-losing-ob-gyns-after-strict-abortion-ban-but-health-exceptions-unlikely-this-year (last accessed June 2024).

21. www.wral.com/bo-s-time-nc-republican-political-newcomer-draws-fire-in-bid-for-toss-up-congressional-seat/20530941/ (last accessed November 2024).

Chapter 1

1. www.jezebel.com/nebraska-teen-sentenced-to-jail-after-abortion-said-she-1850665186 (last accessed June 2024).

2. www.guttmacher.org/article/2016/01/last-five-years-account-more-one-quarter-all-abortion-restrictions-enacted-roe (last accessed June 2024).

3. www.prb.org/Publications/Reports/2017/US-Womens-Well-Being-Stalled.aspx (last accessed June 2024).

4. www.motherjones.com/politics/2017/08/abortion-womens-health-outcomes-maternal-mortality/ (last accessed June 2024).

5. www.guttmacher.org/2024/10/why-six-week-abortion-bans-make-it-impossible-many-people-get-care (last accessed June 2024).

6. www.jezebel.com/mother-charged-with-murder-after-home-birth-in-californ-1850633191 (last accessed June 2024).

7. https://washingtonpost.com/politics/2022/07/09/one-source-story-about-10-year-old-an-abortion-goes-viral/ (last accessed January 2025).

8. www.jezebel.com/8-more-women-join-lawsuit-against-texas-abortion-ban-s-1850462884 (last accessed June 2024).

9. https://jezebel.com/the-horrifying-phenomenon-of-hospitals-detaining-pregna-1850468989?rev=1684957242798 (last accessed June 2024).

10. www.jezebel.com/texas-abortion-ban-lawsuit-1850197371 (last accessed June 2024).

11. www.jezebel.com/kansas-city-health-system-will-no-longer-provide-plan-b-1849124290 (last accessed June 2024).

12. www.jezebel.com/gov-brian-kemp-signals-hes-open-to-banning-plan-b-cont-1849542606 (last accessed June 2024).

13. www.jezebel.com/here-are-the-38-senate-republicans-who-just-blocked-the-right-to-contraception-act (last accessed June 2024).

14. www.jezebel.com/iowa-attorney-general-halts-plan-b-and-abortion-assista-1850317190 (last accessed June 2024).

15. www.jezebel.com/tennessee-republicans-reject-bill-to-protect-ivf-argue-it-would-weaken-abortion-ban (last accessed June 2024).

16. www.jezebel.com/dumb-gop-senate-candidate-says-plan-b-is-used-for-abortion (last accessed October 2024).

17. www.jezebel.com/florida-abortion-ban-six-weeks-rape-exception-proof-1850234075 (last accessed June 2024).

18. www.jezebel.com/abortion-funds-are-spending-astronomical-amounts-of-money-to-help-people-get-care (last accessed June 2024).

Chapter 2

1. www.cbsnews.com/news/beau-rothwell-sentenced-life-in-prison-killing-pregnant-wife-jennifer-rothwell/ (last accessed June 2024).

2. https://jamanetwork.com/journals/jamapsychiatry/fullarticle/ 10.1001/jamapsychiatry.2022.4394?guestAccessKey=9ac07a88-f8d6-40c4-b074-8b1a0311fafo&utm_source=For_The_Media &utm_medium=referral&utm_campaign=ftm_links&utm_content=tfl&utm_term=122822 (last accessed December 2024).

3. www.postandcourier.com/news/special_reports/maternal-death-rate-soars-in-south-carolina/article_797825bd-46ff-59e6-a851-19a0b8106b14.html (last accessed June 2024).

4. https://nationalpartnership.org/report/state-abortion-bans-threaten-black-women/ (last accessed June 2024).

5. www.plannedparenthood.org/learn/abortion/the-abortion-pill/ how-safe-is-the-abortion-pill (last accessed June 2024).

6. https://tcfv.org/wp-content/uploads/TCFV-2022-HTV-Report_ Final-Web.pdf (last accessed December 2024).

7. Same as above. (last accessed June 2024).

8. www.tpr.org/public-health/2024-11-25/domestic-violence-shelters-in-texas-see-a-surge-of-pregnant-women-after-the-dobbs-decision (last accessed December 2024).

9. www.motherjones.com/criminal-justice/2019/11/deval-patrick-spousal-rape-laws/ (last accessed June 2024).

10. https://pubmed.ncbi.nlm.nih.gov/22270271/ (last accessed June 2024).

11. https://jezebel.com/abortion-bans-pregnancy-deaths-1849175032 (last accessed June 2024).

12. https://ci3.uchicago.edu/il-abortion-stats/ (last accessed June 2024).

13. www.washingtonpost.com/politics/2022/07/16/abortion-girl-rape-doctor-bernard-kidnapping-barrett/ (last accessed June 2024).

Chapter 3

1. www.jezebel.com/dont-believe-fearmongering-lawsuits-you-can-leave-your-state-for-an-abortion (last accessed June 2024).

2. www.texastribune.org/2024/05/10/texas-courts-abortion-jonathan-mitchell/ (last accessed June 2024).

3. https://jezebel.com/greg-abbott-pledged-to-eliminate-rape-now-hes-warning-those-who-cross-border-will-be-raped (last accessed June 2024).

4. www.washingtonpost.com/business/2018/10/06/less-than-percent-rapes-lead-felony-convictions-least-percent-victims-face-emotional-physical-consequences (last accessed June 2024).

5. www.salon.com/2017/11/11/86-percent-of-women-in-jail-are-sexual-violence-survivors/ (last accessed June 2024).

6. www.thehotline.org/wp-content/uploads/media/2022/09/2209-Hotline-LES_FINAL.pdf (last accessed June 2024).

7. www.washingtonpost.com/nation/2020/10/17/embrace-black-lives-matter/ (last accessed June 2024).

8. www.huffpost.com/entry/domestic-violence-black-lives-matter-police_n_5f88c8a1c5b66ee9a5ee43d7 (last accessed June 2024).

9. Erica Meiners, Gina Dent, Beth Richie, Angela Davis, *Abolition. Feminism. Now.* (Chicago: Haymarket Books, 2022).

10. www.relevantmagazine.com/current/nation/do-40-percent-of-police-families-really-experience-domestic-abuse/ (last accessed June 2024).

11. https://connect.springerpub.com/highwire_display/entity_view/node/87693/full (last accessed June 2024).

12. https://washingtonpost.com/local/social-issues/a-gendered-trap-when-mothers-allege-child-abuse-by-fathers-the-mothers-often-lose-custody-study-shows/2019/07/28/8f811220-af1d-11e9-bc5c-e73b603e7f38_story.html (last accessed January 2025).

13. https://washingtonpost.com/local/social-issues/a-gendered-trap-when-mothers-allege-child-abuse-by-fathers-the-mothers-often-lose-custody-study-shows/2019/07/28/8f811220-af1d-11e9-bc5c-e73b603e7f38_story.html (last accessed January 2025).

14. www.wnycstudios.org/podcasts/tnyradiohour/segments/custody-conceived-rape?tab=transcript (last accessed June 2024).

15. www.sfchronicle.com/opinion/openforum/article/Open-Forum-abortion-protection-17425633.php (last accessed June 2024).

16. www.nationaladvocatesforpregnantwomen.org/wp-content/uploads/2022/01/FILED-Amicus-Brief-Arizona-Personhood.pdf (last accessed June 2024).

Chapter 4

1. https://norfolkdailynews.com/news/norfolk-woman-19-sentenced-to-jail-and-probation-for-improper-disposal-of-remains/article_1f9352fa-271b-11ee-98a6-f757f5c30aaa.html (last accessed June 2024).

2. www.huffpost.com/entry/texas-abortion-ban-domestic-violence_n_65dcd9a9e4b005b858312158 (last accessed June 2024).

3. https://bmcmedicine.biomedcentral.com/articles/10.1186/s12916-014-0144-z (last accessed June 2024).

4. https://acog.org/clinical/clinical-guidance/committee-opinion/articles/2013/02/reproductive-and-sexual-coercion (last accessed January 2025).

5. www.guttmacher.org/journals/psrh/2012/09/public-health-risks-crisis-pregnancy-centers (last accessed June 2024).

6. www.cbsnews.com/news/abortion-states-have-spent-nearly-500-million-on-anti-abortion-counseling-centers/ (last accessed August 2024).

Chapter 5

1. www.pregnancyjusticeus.org/wp-content/uploads/2023/09/2-Introduction.pdf (last accessed June 2024).

2. https://ifwhenhow.org/resources/selfcare-criminalized/ (last accessed June 2024).

3. www.theguardian.com/us-news/2023/apr/03/pregnancy-birth-murder-charge-kelsey-carpenter-san-diego (last accessed June 2024).

4. www.jezebel.com/public-outrage-may-have-helped-clear-mother-of-murder-charge-over-fatal-home-birth (last accessed June 2024).

5. www.swtimes.com/story/news/state/2017/12/05/district-attorney-oklahoma-county-entities/16903983007/ (last accessed June 2024).

6. www.guttmacher.org/state-policy/explore/substance-use-during-pregnancy (last accessed June 2024).

7. www.samhsa.gov/data/sites/default/files/Spot107AIANAdult CJAdmissions/Spot107AIANAdultCJAdmissions.pdf (last accessed June 2024).

8. www.nicoa.org/census-shows-increase-in-native-population/ (last accessed June 2024).

9. www.ncbi.nlm.nih.gov/pmc/articles/PMC5011980/ (last accessed June 2024).

10. Michele Goodwin, *Policing the Womb*. Cambridge University Press, 2020.

11. https://wearethemeteor.com/tamara-costa-her-life-was-at-risk-alabama-didnt-care/ (last accessed June 2024).

12. https://jezebel.com/abortion-in-the-surveillance-state-1848076906 (last accessed June 2024).

13. http://privacyinternational.org/long-read/3096/how-anti-abortion-activism-exploiting-data (last accessed June 2024).

Chapter 6

1. www.aclu-il.org/sites/default/files/field_documents/expecting_justice_report_3.21.24.pdf (last accessed June 2024).

2. www.rainn.org/statistics/perpetrators-sexual-violence (last accessed June 2024).

3. https://gothamist.com/news/late-night-sex-assaults-invasive-searches-the-700-women-alleging-abuse-at-rikers (last accessed June 2024).

4. www.nytimes.com/2022/11/16/nyregion/new-york-prison-sex-abuse.html (last accessed June 2024).

5. www.ncbi.nlm.nih.gov/pmc/articles/PMC7183903/ (last accessed June 2024).

6. https://revealnews.org/article/female-inmates-sterilized-in-california-prisons-without-approval/ (last accessed June 2024).

Chapter 7

1. https://idahocapitalsun.com/2024/04/05/idaho-is-losing-ob-gyns-after-strict-abortion-ban-but-health-exceptions-unlikely-this-year (last accessed July 2024).

2. https://cidev.uky.edu/kentuckyhealthnews/2024/05/16/15-fewer-med-school-grads-applied-for-residencies-in-kentucky-this-year-med-school-association-attributes-that-to-abortion-ban (last accessed July 2024).

3. www.newsfromthestates.com/article/anti-abortion-researchers-back-riskier-procedures-when-pregnancy-termination-needed-experts (last accessed July 2024).

4. www.npr.org/sections/health-shots/2024/03/19/1239376395/louisiana-abortion-ban-dangerously-disrupting-pregnancy-miscarriage-care (last accessed July 2024).

5. https://scholarlycommons.law.northwestern.edu/cgi/viewcontent.cgi?referer=&httpsredir=1&article=7467&context=jclc (last accessed July 2024).

6. www.ncbi.nlm.nih.gov/pmc/articles/PMC1011231/ (last accessed July 2024).

7. https://damorelaw.com/sexual-abuse-in-hospitals-and-healthcare-facilities/ (last accessed July 2024).

8. www.hhs.gov/about/news/2024/04/01/letter-to-the-nations-teaching-hospitals-and-medical-schools.html (last accessed July 2024).

9. www.news5cleveland.com/news/local-news/investigations/it-felt-like-a-violation-ohio-does-not-require-consent-for-pelvic-exams-on-unconscious-patients (last accessed July 2024).

10. www.cambridge.org/core/journals/american-journal-of-law-and-medicine/article/pelvic-exam-laws-in-the-united-states-a-systematic-review/3165682DE3A5D7C5D487CECD5FF02680 (last accessed July 2024).

Chapter 8

1. https://abcnews.go.com/US/13-year-rape-victim-baby-amid-confusion-states/story?id=108351812 (last accessed July 2024).

2. www.npr.org/2024/10/25/g-s1-28955/abortion-rape-pregnancy-exception-doctor-police-report (last accessed July 2024).

3. https://jezebel.com/missouri-rejects-rape-exceptions-senator-says-forced-b-1851239306 (last accessed July 2024); https://jezebel.

com/gop-lawmakers-in-louisiana-reject-adding-rape-incest-exceptions-for-children-to-abortion-ban-again (last accessed July 2024); https://jezebel.com/indiana-is-latest-to-try-to-criminalize-abortion-pills-also-targets-rape-exception-abortion-funds (last accessed July 2024).

4. www.nbcnews.com/think/opinion/abortion-exceptions-rape-dont-ensure-victims-rape-me-can-ncna1012176 (last accessed July 2024).

Chapter 9

1. https://static.project2025.org/2025_MandateForLeadership_FULL.pdf (last accessed July 2024).
2. www.axios.com/2024/03/29/abortion-pill-supreme-court-case-poll (last accessed July 2024).
3. www.ohchr.org/en/statements/2024/02/gaza-when-mothers-have-bury-least-7700-children-very-basic-principles-are (last accessed December 2024).
4. https://jezebel.com/miscarriages-in-gaza-have-increased-300-under-israeli-1851168680 (last accessed July 2024).
5. https://jezebel.com/pregnant-women-in-gaza-are-undergoing-c-sections-withou-1850982366 (last accessed July 2024).
6. https://arc-southeast.org/2023/10/24/rj-includes-palestine/ (last accessed July 2024).
7. https://jezebel.com/planned-parenthood-employees-say-they-re-left-to-clean-1851095985 (last accessed July 2024).
8. https://swampland.time.com/2009/05/21/vatican-newspaper-obama-is-not-a-pro-abortion-president/ (last accessed July 2024).
9. www.politico.com/news/2024/06/09/aipac-republican-donors-democratic-primaries-00162404 (last accessed November 2024).

Conclusion

1. www.hrw.org/news/2024/07/03/dominican-republics-senate-doubles-down-abortion-ban-criminal-code (last accessed July 2024).

2. https://rewirenewsgroup.com/2024/05/09/under-brazils-abortion-ban-lack-of-information-kills/ (last accessed July 2024).

3. https://notesfrompoland.com/2022/01/26/woman-dies-in-poland-after-being-made-to-carry-dead-foetus-for-seven-days/ (last accessed July 2024).

4. www.jezebel.com/poland-which-bans-nearly-all-abortions-has-created-a-1849028586 (last accessed July 2024).

5. www.telegraph.co.uk/news/2023/07/27/poland-police-search-sewage-system-foetus-lying-miscarriage/ (last accessed July 2024).

6. www.nytimes.com/2023/09/14/opinion/abortion-pills-testing-poland.html (last accessed July 2024).

7. www.theguardian.com/global-development/2022/mar/28/polish-woman-is-first-to-face-trial-for-violating-strict-abortion-law (last accessed August 2024).

The Pluto Press Newsletter

Hello friend of Pluto!

Want to stay on top of the best radical books
we publish?

Then sign up to be the first to hear about our
new books, as well as special events,
podcasts and videos.

You'll also get 50% off your first order with us
when you sign up.

Come and join us!

Go to bit.ly/PlutoNewsletter